The Art of the Party

The Art of the Party

Drinks & Nibbles for Easy Entertaining

KAY PLUNKETT-HOGGE

MITCHELL BEAZLEY

As always, for Fred.
The gin to my vermouth.

CONTENTS

INTRODUCTION

I love a party. I love a good bar and an icy cocktail. I have been privileged enough to have worked in two industries (fashion and film) where canapés make up a major food group. I believe that delicious, bite-sized food and well-made drinks are a force for good. And I've written three books to argue the point. So it's important to tell you up front that this new volume is a compilation, the Greatest Hits album if you will, derived from the titles that came before.

However, any decent Greatest Hits record has got to have at least a new single or two, something you can't find anywhere else. And to that end, I've squeezed in a dozen new recipes to keep this honest.

What this book really does is bring together my philosophy of entertaining friends in small groups or large, which boils down to this. If you're going to entertain, the first person who needs to have a good time is… you. If you're stressed out, or you've taken on too much, you're going to be miserable, and consequently your guests will be, too.

Add an H and an E to the art of the party, and you have the heart of the party: the host or hostess. You.

Throwing a party should involve minimal fuss and maximum enjoyment. The drinks you make and the food you serve should reflect what you like, and how you like to have fun. That's why people are coming round to yours. Because no one throws a shindig quite like you do.

So whip out that little black dress, steam the creases out of your sharpest suit, crank up the music and cut loose. If there's plenty to drink and something to eat, you can't go wrong. It's supposed to be a party, after all.

Party Basics

THE ART OF THE PARTY

Throwing a good party should be enormous fun, both for your guests and for you. Here are some simple tips to help things go with a swing.

PLANNING

This is what it all comes down to. The more you can prepare ahead of time, the easier your evening will be. For a start, you'll feel more relaxed and so will your friends. The problem is that so many of us suffer from performance anxiety when it comes to entertaining and, really, we shouldn't. After all, everyone you've invited is meant to be a friend, so what can go wrong?

DRINKS

It doesn't matter how many people you've invited, the fact of it is that you don't run a bar and won't have every kind of liquor or elixir stuffed into a cupboard, so the whole gamut of cocktails is out of the question. Offer a couple of options, and wine and beer if you feel like it. If you have a large number of guests, by which I mean more than 20, it's a good idea to choose a drink you can scale up and premix.

SCALING UP

A lot of cocktail recipes can be restructured so that you think about their ingredients in terms of ratios instead of measurements. This makes it very much easier to scale them up for a party. For example, the Margarita (see page 42) works out as one part lime juice to one part triple sec to two parts tequila (1:1:2). So before anyone arrives, you can premix a perfect batch of cocktails to those proportions, beginning with the ingredient of which you have the least (usually the lime juice), and then shake them over ice for your guests as required. **Here are some cocktails that scale up beautifully:**

The Margarita (see page 42)

The Cosmopolitan (see page 20) – just add the dash of cranberry juice as you shake each one

The Fine and Dandy (see page 21)

The Negroni (see page 24)

The Whiskey Sour (see page 26)

The Shirley Temple (see page 53)

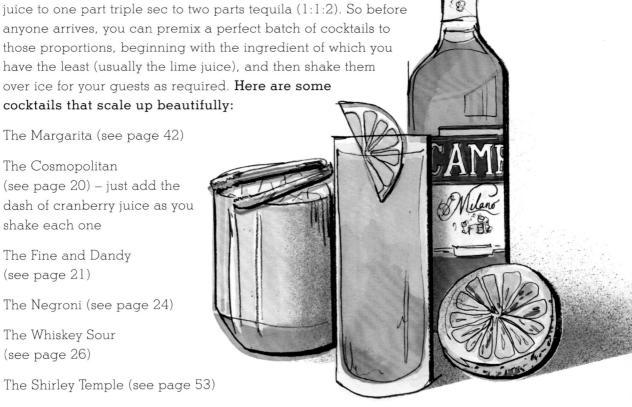

FOOD

Again, keep it simple. Never forget that your friends have come round to see you, so it's not going to be the ideal evening if you never leave the kitchen! The snacks need to be substantial enough to stop people from feeling the effects of the cocktails TOO much, and they need to go with the setting – if it's an evening where everyone's on their feet, you want food that's easy to hold and isn't going to drip down somebody's frock. If it's a smaller affair, or a brunch, then plates and forks (oh, how I do love a cocktail fork!) can come out, and the food can be a little more robust.

The important thing is to make sure you serve things that reflect the numbers you've invited. The more people, the simpler you want it to be. If there are just eight of you, then you might want to cook a few things that take a bit of time. If there are 28, you'd probably prefer to serve something less arduous to prepare. So choose your canapés accordingly.

HOW MUCH IS ENOUGH?

Here are a few tips to make the question of how much to feed and water the masses a little easier:

For wine or bubbly, half a bottle per person is fairly standard. I have a deep-set fear of running out, so I always veer toward three-quarters to a bottle per person and know I'll have leftovers. Most wine merchants will sell wine by the case on sale or return. Just be careful not to ice all the white wine or Champagne because they won't accept it back if you soak off the labels.

I generally estimate two to three cocktails an hour per head, plus one for luck! Bear in mind that most people will slow down as the evening goes on.

Always have plenty of still and sparkling water on hand and at least one non-alcoholic drink.

If the party is to last 2 hours, bank on 8–10 canapés per head, of perhaps 3–5 different types.

For 3 hours, go for 12–14 canapés per head, of perhaps 6–8 different types.

For 4 hours plus – well, at this point you can echo my father: "I invited you for drinks, not for breakfast." At which point he'd ring a large ship's bell. You can just smile and say the party is over.

If you are serving pre-dinner drinks, however, I think 4–5 canapés per head is fine: you want your guests to have room for their dinner! In fact, I often just serve Salted Almonds (see page 115) and a Soup Shot (see pages 94–97) if we're heading into a substantial meal.

So let's shake up some cocktails and stir up some trouble. After all, it's meant to be a party!

BEFORE, DURING AND AFTER

I don't want to preach, but here are a few tips that I've found invaluable.

Make sure you take into account who you're inviting and why. If it's a party to welcome your new boss, it's going to be a very different affair to one that marks the start of the football season. Extreme comparisons I know, but you get the drift.

Casting: don't invite two feuding ex-lovers, especially to a smaller affair. Likewise anyone you know who, God forbid, is a mean drunk. Bigger parties have fewer issues, as everyone can mix and mingle without ruffling feathers.

Unless you intend on hiring extra help, I wouldn't advise going much above the 25–30 guest mark at home. You want to enjoy yourself rather than plan a full-scale military exercise!

Do enlist family and friends to help: most people love to be useful.

Regardless of the occasion, make sure you invite your guests in a timely fashion. I don't mean sending an official embossed card posted months before the event, but three weeks' notice is good. It gives you time to get organized, too. If you want to have a dress code, make sure your guests know in advance to avoid embarrassment. Ask if they have any dietary needs or allergies.

Will people be driving? While your guests' sobriety is not (entirely) your responsibility, I think it's a courtesy to make sure there's a solid non-alcoholic alternative if you know people are coming by car. And do supply phone numbers for local taxi services.

Think about whether you need to rent glasses and plates. Have the liquor delivered as well, if you can, to save time.

Ice, ice, baby…Make sure there's PLENTY of it. Have some tubs (or baby bathtubs) at the ready to receive it!

Décor – or un-décor: if you've invited more than a handful of guests, then think about clearing some space for food, for drinks, for shimmying and mingling. Pop away anything that's fragile or precious… or precarious. And beware of lit candles when the drinks are flowing.

Make it VERY clear whether there are smoking areas or not.

Fresh flowers, space and a smile are the best decoration. I tend to advise against "themes". It's a party, not a party game.

Don't forget to HOST! If everyone there already knows everyone else, then fine, things can take care of themselves. If not, well, I know you'll be busy, but be sure to introduce people. It's the one thing everyone forgets, and it's the one thing that makes sure everyone has a good time. If you see someone alone while you're busy frying croquettes, send a gregarious friend over to help them mingle.

And finally, after the event: don't wash the glasses until the morning (BR-EAK-AGE!!). That tip is from my wonderful mama!

The Drinks

THE MARTINI

The food writer M F K Fisher once said that the Martini is to America what vodka is to Russia. Hemingway said they made him feel civilized. I say they are **the perfect antidote to rainy days** (literally or figuratively) – to quote Mae West, I like to get out of my wet clothes and into a Dry Martini. No other cocktail inspires more comment or opinion. *Should it be shaken? Should it be stirred?* Should it be gin or should it be vodka? And how much vermouth is too much vermouth?

Throwing myself into the Martini melee, I should point out that the opinions below are merely my own. They're also right. So don't argue.

Shaken or stirred is a matter of preference. I prefer mine stirred to the point where it's as cold as the bottom of a penguin's foot. If you shake it, you will break the ice cubes and make a cloudy and more diluted drink. I think that a Martini's ice-cold clarity is a big part of its charm.

A Martini is made with gin. A Vodka Martini is made with vodka. Apple Martinis are an abomination. That is all.

An olive or a twist is also a matter of preference, but the twist should always be lemon – if you want lime, order a Gimlet and be done with it – and unwaxed. The olive should be vividly green and unstuffed. If you like it "dirty" – with a splash of the olive brine – be as dirty as you please.

I don't care that Noël Coward thought it sufficient to wave the shaker in the general direction of Italy – there must be vermouth. This is a mixed drink: without the vermouth, it's not a Martini. It's just a glass of cold gin.

The ice must be fresh. The longer it's in your freezer, the more it picks up residual flavours. With the Martini, we're shooting for drinking perfection. We'll never make it, but we were born to try.

This is how I make mine...

Fill a cocktail shaker with fresh ice. Pour in a dash of dry vermouth – we're talking no more than $\frac{1}{8}$ of a teaspoonful. I favour Noilly Prat, but Dolin is also excellent. Stir vigorously to coat the ice cubes thoroughly. Pour a cocktail-glassful of gin into the shaker. Stir, stir, stir until it's as cold as a politician's soul. Leave to rest while you spear your olives on to a cocktail stick or cut your twist from your lemon. Strain into the glass, garnish and serve at once, ideally with Salted Almonds (see page 115) and a side of insouciance.

Salted Almonds

PAGE 115

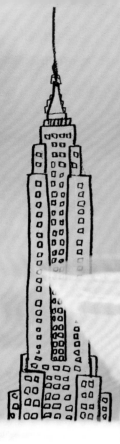

THE COSMOPOLITAN

There's a misconception about the Cosmopolitan: people assume that, because it's pink, it should be sweet. Ideally, a Cosmopolitan should be **tart, with a sweet back**. It was reinvented by the legendary Toby Cecchini, who used to run the equally legendary bar Passerby (one of my favourites), when he worked at The Odeon in New York (another of my favourites) in the late 1980s. If ever a drink conquered a city, this was it. *Honour is due.*

MAKES 1

25ml (1fl oz) vodka

25ml (1fl oz) triple sec

20ml (¾fl oz) fresh lime juice

a splash of cranberry juice (just to stain the drink, no more)

a twist of lemon, to garnish

Fill a cocktail shaker with ice. Add the liquid ingredients and shake like hell. Pour into a chilled Martini glass and garnish with a fat twist of lemon.

THE FINE AND DANDY

The Fine and Dandy is a bit of a forgotten gem. It's fresh and sophisticated, and its peachy hue is a delight to behold. However, I cannot find out where it came from. Since every cocktail should have an origin story, here goes mine. *Fine and Dandy* was a show written in 1930 by Kay Swift, the first woman to score a full Broadway musical. It was a massive hit, and its title number was covered by everyone from Charlie Parker to Barbra Streisand. So I'm going to stick my neck out and say the drink was named for it. On a side note, Kay Swift eloped with a rodeo cowboy in 1939. *She sounds like my kind of girl.*

MAKES 1

20ml (¾fl oz) fresh lemon juice

20ml (¾fl oz) Cointreau

40ml (1¼fl oz) gin

a dash of Angostura bitters

Fill a cocktail shaker with ice and add all the ingredients. Shake until icy cold and strain into a Martini glass.

Kay's Tip...

Some people garnish this with a maraschino cherry. I feel it's better without. Either way, sup with Peggy Lee's recording playing in the background.

GIN AND IT

Short for "**gin and Italian**", this dates back at least as far as my beloved Martini. Which makes sense – early versions of the Martini were very much "wetter" than those we serve today, and of similar proportions to this. Perhaps that's one of the reasons why it fell out of favour in recent years. But with more and more sweet vermouths available, there is every reason to revisit it. The smooth Italian of the vermouth just sidles up to kiss the very British gin and make her blush. *Sophisticated and slick, this drink has a kick.*

MAKES 1

60ml (2¼fl oz) gin

30ml (1fl oz) red vermouth

1–2 dashes of orange bitters

a twist of lemon, to garnish

Stir the gin and vermouth together over ice and strain into a cocktail glass, or pour the spirits over some ice in a rocks glass. Add the orange bitters. Stir. Garnish with a lemon twist.

THE AMERICANO

Ah, the Americano – the chic, sophisticated precursor of the magnificent Negroni. It is balanced and light, and **simple enough to make in batches for a party**. It is not a cup of coffee.

MAKES 1

30ml (1fl oz) red vermouth

30ml (1fl oz) Campari

soda water, to top up

a slice or a twist of orange, to garnish

Pour the vermouth and Campari into a rocks glass filled with ice. Top up with soda water and stir gently. Garnish with an orange slice or twist.

THE NEGRONI

This is alleged to have been invented in Florence by Count Negroni, who asked the bartender at the Hotel Baglioni to strengthen his Americano with a spot of gin, but no one knows if this is actually true. **Orson Welles was one of the first Americans to write about it**, saying "the bitters are excellent for your liver, the gin is bad for you. They balance each other out." James Bond orders one in the short story "Risico". So consider it *a drink endorsed by proper drinkers.*

MAKES 1

20ml (¾fl oz) gin

20ml (¾fl oz) Campari

20ml (¾fl oz) red vermouth

a slice or a twist of orange, to garnish

Pour the gin, Campari and red vermouth over 3–4 ice cubes in a tumbler. Stir the spirits together until they are very cold. Garnish with a slice or twist of orange, ideally a blood orange.

Kay's Tip...

If you leave out the gin, and top with prosecco, you get a Negroni Sbagliato, or a Wrong Negroni.

THE WHISKEY SOUR

You can make a classic Sour with any spirit you like, to the proportions below. The trick is balancing the lemon and sugar to achieve the perfect lip-puckering proportions that make this drink truly satisfying – some lemons are sourer than others. I sometimes like to make this with Meyer lemons if I can find them. And when I can't and I'm looking for that flavour, I replace 5–10ml (1–2 teaspoons) of the lemon juice with freshly squeezed orange juice to find the proper tang. *Delicious!*

SUGAR SYRUP

You can buy sugar syrup in bottles, but it is easy to make at home and considerably cheaper. Simply measure out equal quantities of caster sugar and water – say 250ml (9fl oz) water to 250g (9oz) sugar – into a saucepan. Then dissolve the sugar completely in the water over a low heat (the heat isn't strictly necessary; it just speeds up the process). Leave to cool, then store in a sterilized bottle for up to one month in the fridge.

MAKES 1

50ml (2fl oz) bourbon or blended Scotch whisky

20ml (¾fl oz) fresh lemon juice

20ml (¾fl oz) Sugar Syrup (see left)

To garnish

a slice of lemon

a maraschino cherry (optional)

Pour all the ingredients into a cocktail shaker with plenty of ice and shake until cold. Strain into a Sour glass and serve garnished with a slice of lemon and a maraschino cherry, if you like.

Kay's Tip...

You can also serve this on the rocks, either in a tumbler or Old Fashioned glass.

THE BICICLETTA

According to urban legend, the Bicicletta is named after a poor chap who after a few too many *aperitivi* rode his bike home rather erratically... True or not, the image does make me smile. It is a **refreshing and simple** drink to make – after a couple, however, *I'd recommend that you park the bike and walk home.*

MAKES 1

50ml (2fl oz) Campari

50ml (2fl oz) dry white wine

soda water, to top up

a slice of lemon, to garnish

Stir the Campari and white wine together in a large wine glass. Add ice and top up with soda water. Garnish with a slice of lemon.

THE OLD FASHIONED

Along with the Swizzle, the Old Fashioned is pretty much ground zero for the cocktail, dating back to at least 1806. And although there are numerous variations on the recipe, **the essentials of the drink have hardly changed**. All you need is sugar, bitters and hard liquor. And, as I'm an old-fashioned girl, *this is my kind of drink*.

MAKES 1

1 sugar cube

a few dashes of Angostura bitters, to taste

60–80ml (2¼–2¾fl oz) bourbon or rye whiskey

To garnish

a wedge or a twist of orange

a maraschino cherry (optional)

Place the sugar cube in the bottom of a tumbler and saturate it with a few dashes of Angostura bitters, to taste. Crush the sugar and the bitters together with a muddler – some people like to add a dash of water at this point to help the sugar dissolve. Then add a few large cubes of ice. Pour in the bourbon or rye and stir briefly to amalgamate. Garnish with the orange and a maraschino cherry, if you like.

Kay's Tip...

One of the best Old Fashioneds I have had was made with baconized bourbon. To make it, buy the smokiest cure of streaky bacon you can find – hickory smoked is best – and cook up enough for a good bacon sandwich. While it's cooking, pour 350ml (12fl oz) bourbon into a clean jam jar. When the bacon's done, make your sandwich – you can't let it go to waste – then pour the bacon fat into the jar with the bourbon. You should have a good 2–3 tablespoons. Leave to steep for a day, then put the jar into the freezer until the bacon fat has completely solidified. Strain through a coffee filter paper into a clean, sterilized bottle. The bourbon should now look like, well, bourbon, but it will have a distinct smoky bacon aroma. Delicious!

THE SPRITZ

As with so many drinks, the Spritz's story dates back to the late 19th and early 20th centuries, depending on which story you choose to believe, when one could find a lot of Austrian soldiers wandering around the Veneto. They didn't like the local wine, and took to adding soda water to punch up its acidity. Hence "spritz", which derives from the German word *spritzen*, "to spray".

The modern Aperol Spritz we know and love today was created at the Bar Capannina in Lido di Jesolo, Venice, in the mid-1990s. In a larger glass, they combined Aperol, prosecco and ice to immediate success. Such success, in fact, that Aperol has geared its entire brand marketing around it. And to such success that we are forced to ask: can a Spritz be a Spritz without it?

Much as I love Aperol, the answer has to be "yes". What is the Negroni Sbagliato (see page 25) if not some sort of a Spritz? In addition to Aperol, there's the old and glorious standby Campari, Martini Bitter, Contratto Bitter, Berto Aperitivo, Punt e Mes (which manages to blend the genres of bitter, vermouth and amaro into one very sexy bottle) and so on.

In fact, so successful has Aperol been at reviving this sector of the booze biz that long-lost brands are beginning to re-emerge, like the saffron-hued Villacidro from Sardinia, first produced in 1882 and now reborn after falling cataclysmically from local fashion.

So, whether you mix bitter with prosecco or you take the more traditional approach and use bitter, soda water and white wine, there is now a host of products with which to fix your Spritz. As ever, the key is experimentation. Any good bartender worth their salt will let you have a whiff or a taste of a drink that you don't recognize (all the better to show off their latest discovery; all the better to sell you some). It all just depends on whatever bittersweet mood you're in tonight.

MAKES 1

60ml (2¼fl oz) Aperol or Campari

120ml (4fl oz) prosecco

60ml (2¼fl oz) soda water

To garnish

1–2 large, shiny green olives

a wedge of orange

Fill a large wine goblet with ice. Pour in the Aperol or Campari. Pour in the prosecco and top up with soda water. Garnish with an olive, or 2 if you like, and the orange.

THE POINSETTIA

This is an **ideal party cocktail**, especially in the winter, since it's the same festive colour as the plant it takes its name from. Why? Because you don't need to shake anything (if you did, the fizz would explode all over the house), you don't need to stir anything (you'll lose all the bubbles), you don't even need to worry about ice. *Just make sure everything is cold from the fridge.*

TO MAKE 1

30ml (1fl oz) chilled cranberry juice

15ml (½fl oz) chilled Cointreau

chilled English sparkling wine or prosecco, to top up

a twist of orange or a fresh cranberry, to garnish

Pour the cranberry juice and Cointreau into a Champagne flute. Top up with sparkling wine and garnish with a twist of orange or a cranberry.

TO MAKE ABOUT 10

750ml (1¼ pints) chilled English sparkling wine or prosecco

375ml (13fl oz) chilled cranberry juice

100ml (3½fl oz) chilled Cointreau

10 twists of orange or fresh cranberries, to garnish

Pour all the ingredients into a big jug, then pour into Champagne flutes and garnish each with a twist of orange or a cranberry.

THE CLASSIC CHAMPAGNE COCKTAIL

Known by some, back in the day, as **Chorus Girls' Milk**, the Champagne Cocktail is one of the oldest going. Recipes date back deep into the 1800s. This version, though, probably emerged sometime in the early 1890s, but no one is entirely sure. The brandy, ideally Cognac, is optional, and its quantity is a matter of taste. In **The Big Sleep**, General Sternwood preferred it to make up one-third of the drink. In **Casablanca**, neither Victor Laszlo nor Captain Renault seemed to care. So it's really up to you. This is the **perfect celebratory cocktail – what's a party without fizz**?

MAKES 1

1 sugar cube

3–4 dashes of Angostura or Peychaud's bitters

Cognac, to cover the sugar cube

chilled Champagne, to top up

a twist of orange, to garnish

Put the sugar in the bottom of a Champagne flute and douse it with the bitters. Pour in enough Cognac to cover the sugar, then top up carefully with Champagne, remembering that the bitters will make the Champagne fizz more than usual. Finally, squeeze the oils from a piece of orange peel over the surface of the drink, then add the twist and serve.

Kay's Tip...

If you have time (or freezer space), chill the glasses before you make the drink.

THE GIN FIZZ

The Fizz, the Collins and the Sour are closely related. Each involves a similar blend of lemon juice, sugar and spirit, then the recipes deviate. In essence, a Fizz is a shaken Sour that is topped up with soda water. And a Collins is a stirred Sour that is…topped up with soda water. Does it make a difference? Generations of bartenders say so. I suggest that they are both equally refreshing and equally delicious.

MAKES 1

25ml (1fl oz) fresh lemon juice

50ml (2fl oz) gin

10ml (2 teaspoons) Sugar Syrup (see page 26)

chilled soda water, to top up

To make the Fizz, fill a cocktail shaker with ice and pour in the lemon juice, gin and sugar syrup. Shake hard until ice-cold. Strain into an ice-filled highball glass and top up with soda water.

You can substitute the gin with rye or bourbon, or with Nick Cuthbert's Sloe Gin (see opposite). You can also replace the lemon juice with Meyer lemon juice, which is slightly sweeter, to make a Meyer Lemon Fizz.

Kay's Tip…

To make your Fizz into a Collins, fill a Collins glass with ice and pour in the lemon juice, gin and sugar syrup. Stir well to combine, then top up with soda water. Garnish with a twist of lemon and a maraschino cherry.

NICK CUTHBERT'S SLOE GIN FIZZ

Sloes are at their best for picking after the first frost. But Nick says why wait? Just put them in the freezer for a day, then defrost them before making the sloe gin.

MAKES 1

20ml (¾fl oz) Sloe Gin (see below)

100ml (3½fl oz) chilled prosecco or English sparkling wine

TO MAKE 750ML (1¼ PINTS) SLOE GIN

500g (1lb 2oz) sloes, frozen and then defrosted

750ml (1¼ pints) gin

300g (10½oz) sugar

To make the sloe gin, mix all the ingredients together in a large jar or screw-top bottle and leave for 1–3 months in a cool, dark place. Be sure to give the bottle a good shake every day. When it's done, strain it into a sterilized bottle. It will keep indefinitely.

To make the cocktail, pour the sloe gin into a glass and top up with the prosecco or English sparkling wine.

THE FRENCH 75

Is this a gin cocktail or a Champagne cocktail? I say gin, but either way it's said to have the **kick of a French 75mm field gun**. This was created by Harry MacElhone of Harry's Bar, New York, in 1915. It definitely packs a punch – *you have been warned*!

MAKES 1

40ml (1¼fl oz) gin

20ml (¾fl oz) fresh lemon juice

10–20ml (2–4 teaspoons) Sugar Syrup (see page 26)

chilled Champagne, to top up

a twist of lemon, to garnish

Fill a cocktail shaker with ice and add the gin, lemon juice and sugar syrup to taste. Shake well, then strain into a Champagne flute. Top up with Champagne and garnish with a twist of lemon.

THE BELLINI

The Bellini originates from Harry's Bar, in Venice. Some people make this with Champagne, some people use nectarines. They are wrong. **It must be made with peaches and prosecco**. *Accept no substitutes*.

MAKES 1

2 tablespoons freshly pulped peaches, preferably white ones

chilled prosecco, to top up

Spoon the peach pulp into the bottom of a glass and top up carefully with prosecco. I say carefully, because the peach will make it fizz up even more than usual, something that has often caught me out! Stir briefly to lift the peach into the drink, and serve.

Kay's Tip...

You can easily create Bellinis in batches – simply spoon the peach pulp into glasses, and just keep pouring until the prosecco runs dry.

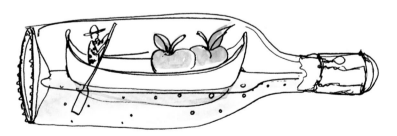

THE BLOODY MARY BAR

There's nothing quite like an icy, spicy Bloody Mary, and it can be **a fun addition to a party** – make a classic drink as per the recipe below, then *let your guests customize their cocktail by adding something – or everything – from the Bloody Mary Bar*!

MAKES 1

60ml (2¼fl oz) vodka

½ teaspoon grated horseradish

Tabasco sauce, to taste

Worcestershire sauce, to taste

a wedge of lemon

chilled tomato juice, to top up

celery salt and freshly ground black pepper

Fill a highball glass with ice. Pour in the vodka. Season with a good pinch of celery salt and several grinds of black pepper. Add the horseradish and several dashes of Tabasco and Worcestershire sauce (the more the merrier in my book). Squeeze in the lemon wedge and top up with tomato juice. Stir and serve, letting your guest choose what to add from the bar options.

Bloody Mary Bar Options

- Pickled chillies on sticks
- Dill pickles, quartered
- Oysters on the half-shell
- Sticks of salsify
- Sticks of celery and whole, long carrots
- Cooked prawns on skewers
- Stuffed olives on sticks
- Strips of crispy bacon
- A selection of hot sauces

THE MARGARITA

When I lived in Los Angeles, the Margarita was **my drink of choice** – it was one of my Five-a-Day. I was a terror: I used to go to the Formosa Cafe at about half past one in the morning, steal the keys as the owner Vince was locking up and force him to make me one. I'd always order another, so in the end he served them to me in a pint glass so he could clean down in peace – something that has proved a solid basis for a life-long friendship.

As to the drink itself, it was either created by Carlos Orozco at Hussong's Cantina in Ensenada, in Baja California, in 1941 and named for the daughter of the German ambassador, or it was invented by bartender Santos Cruz at the Balinese Room in Galveston, Texas, in 1948 and named for Peggy Lee (Peggy being short for Margaret, hence Margarita).

It's a great drink for parties and can easily be scaled up and made in advance.

MAKES 1

a wedge of lime

30ml (1fl oz) fresh lime juice

30ml (1fl oz) Cointreau or other triple sec

60ml (2¼fl oz) white tequila

fine sea salt flakes

Wipe the lime wedge around the rim of a tumbler, then dip the rim in salt to coat it. Fill a cocktail shaker with ice and add the lime juice, triple sec and tequila. Shake rhythmically to Peggy Lee's "Fever" until very cold. Fill the tumbler with fresh ice, then strain the drink over the top. Squeeze in the wedge of lime, add it to the drink and serve.

Kay's Tip...

To make a Frozen Margarita, place the tequila, lime juice and triple sec in a blender with plenty of ice. Blitz until smooth, then serve in a salt-rimmed glass.

SANGRIA

The idea of flavouring wine goes back to the Romans. And since they, allegedly, took vines to Spain, it seems apt that **Spain is where this flavoured wine originates**. Almost every bar or restaurant has its own version. In southern Spain, they make a variation called *zurra*, which uses peaches – so *feel free to play around with different fruits and different sweetnesses to make the drink your own*.

SERVES 6–8

750ml (1¼ pints) red wine

2 lemons, cut into wedges

1 orange, cut into wedges

2–3 tablespoons caster sugar

30ml (1fl oz) Grand Marnier or aged orange Curaçao

75ml (2½fl oz) Spanish brandy

500ml (18fl oz) chilled soda water

Mix the wine, fruit, sugar, Grand Marnier or Curaçao and brandy together in a jug. Cover and leave to steep for at least an hour, but no more than 6.

When you're ready to serve, add the soda water and pour into ice-filled glasses.

Potato, Manchego and Saffron Tortilla

PAGE 169

HOT BUTTERED RUM

There's nothing more warming or more soothing than a mug of hot buttered rum... This drink is as *resolutely unfashionable as a Christmas jumper, but just as welcome at the right moment*!

MAKES 1

30g (1oz) Spiced Butter (see right)

60ml (2¼fl oz) aged or dark rum

freshly boiled water, to top up

freshly grated nutmeg, to garnish

For the Spiced Butter

(FOR 8–10 DRINKS)

200g (7oz) dark soft brown sugar

125g (4½oz) unsalted butter, softened

¾ teaspoon freshly grated nutmeg

1½ teaspoons ground allspice

2 pinches of ground mace

a pinch of ground cinnamon

a pinch of salt

To make the spiced butter, put all the ingredients in a mixing bowl and mix together. Turn out on to a sheet of clingfilm and wrap tightly. The spiced butter will keep in the fridge for up to 1 month, or you can freeze it.

   To make the drink, put the spiced butter in a mug and add the rum. Top up with freshly boiled water and stir until the butter has melted and emulsified into the drink. Garnish with a grating of nutmeg.

Kay's Tip...

There is a quicker version. Dissolve 1 teaspoon sugar in a little boiling water in a mug. Add a good slug of rum and 30g (1oz) butter. Top up with more hot water and grate some nutmeg over the top. Job done.

MRS BROWNE'S EGGNOG

This comes from a handwritten recipe book belonging to Granny Alice, my husband's Jamaican great-grandmother. I've had to adapt it slightly to update it, but *it's serious, potent, rich and, well, glorious*.

SERVES 6–8

2–3 tablespoons Sugar Syrup (see page 26)

1 egg

125ml (4fl oz) Cognac

65ml (2¼fl oz) dark rum, preferably Appleton

chilled milk, to top up

freshly grated nutmeg, to garnish

Pour the sugar syrup into a cocktail shaker, add the egg and the spirits and shake until the ingredients are well emulsified. Pour into a pint glass.

Put 4–5 ice cubes in a blender and blitz until they have the texture of snow. If a couple of the cubes are still solid, don't worry. Scoop the ice into the pint glass and top up with milk. Return everything to the blender and blitz again to mix thoroughly.

Pour out into eggnog or punch cups, holding back the foam but making sure everyone gets some. Garnish with freshly grated nutmeg.

Kay's Tip...

Granny Alice says that, to make a hot version, one simply replaces the ice with boiling water.

GLÖGG

Glögg is the **Scandinavian version of mulled wine** – an essential component of the run-up to Christmas. Recipes vary from country to country. This one was given to my parents by a friend who ran the ground operation for SAS in Bangkok back in the day, so Glögg became an essential component of the Plunkett Christmas, too. Some recipes suggest making it a week in advance to allow all the flavours to develop fully. I've never done this. Mainly because *it smells so good we tend to drink it as soon as it's made*.

SERVES 10–12

700ml (1¼ pints) vodka

750ml (1¼ pints) robust red wine

5 cardamom pods, cracked open

5 whole cloves

1 cinnamon stick

a piece of orange peel

a 4cm (1½-inch) piece of fresh root ginger, peeled and roughly sliced

250g (9oz) caster sugar

a large handful each of raisins and blanched almonds, to serve

Mix together all the ingredients except the raisins and almonds and leave for 2–4 hours.

Pour the mixture into a saucepan and heat slowly. Do not allow to boil.

Strain out the spices, then pour into glass cups or mugs. Add the raisins and almonds just before serving.

THREE LEMONADES

There's **nothing more refreshing** than a cold glass of lemonade. So here are three of them – *I call that refreshment [ice] cubed*!

CLASSIC LEMONADE

SERVES 8–10

175g (6oz) caster sugar

225ml (8fl oz) water

350ml (12fl oz) fresh lemon juice (about 6–8 lemons)

1 litre (1¾ pints) chilled water

Place the sugar and the 225ml (8fl oz) water in a saucepan over a medium heat and stir until the sugar has completely dissolved. Do not allow to boil. Pour it into a heatproof measuring jug and leave to cool. Pour half the syrup into a jug. Add the lemon juice and chilled water and taste the lemonade, adding more of the syrup if it is too sharp for your taste. Serve over ice in highball glasses.

Kay's Tip...

The simple syrup here is not as sweet as the one on page 26. This is a matter of taste, and to balance out the refreshing sour-sweet zing of a lemonade. If you'd like to add more sugar, it's entirely up to you.

RASPBERRY LEMONADE

SERVES 10

300g (10½oz) raspberries

175g (6oz) caster sugar

225ml (8fl oz) water

350ml (12fl oz) fresh lemon juice
(about 6–8 lemons)

1 litre (1¾ pints) chilled water

Rub the raspberries through a
fine sieve using a wooden spoon,
then discard the pips. Follow the
method for Classic Lemonade
(see opposite) to make the sugar
syrup. When the syrup has cooled,
mix it with the raspberry purée
and the lemon juice, then top up
with the chilled water. Serve over
ice in highball glasses.

BASIL AND MINT LEMONADE

SERVES 8–10

1 quantity of Classic Lemonade
(see opposite)

20g (¾oz) basil leaves

20g (¾oz) mint leaves

Make the Classic Lemonade
(see opposite), then pour into
a blender and tear in the basil
and mint leaves. Blend until almost
smooth, then strain through a fine
sieve into a jug. Serve over ice in
highball glasses.

THE RUDE BOI

I came up with this for my nephews Alex and Alastair when they were younger. Originally we used Lilt, a pineapple-flavoured fizzy drink, instead of ginger beer because they loved it. If anything, it makes the drink sweeter than it is already!

MAKES 1

60ml (2¼fl oz) shop-bought mango and passion fruit smoothie

30ml (1fl oz) Sugar Syrup (see page 26)

chilled ginger beer, to top up

a slice of orange or a maraschino cherry, to garnish

Fill a Collins glass with ice. Pour in the smoothie and the sugar syrup and top up with chilled ginger beer. Stir together, garnish with a slice of orange or a maraschino cherry and serve at once.

THE SHIRLEY TEMPLE

This was allegedly invented in the late 1930s for the child star at Chasen's, Beverly Hills. Or the Brown Derby. Or the Royal Hawaiian. (They were all in on the act!) She has said, apparently, she never liked it much.

MAKES 1

chilled ginger ale or 7 Up, or an equal mix of both

a dash of grenadine

a maraschino cherry, to garnish

Fill a glass with ice cubes and pour in ginger ale or 7 Up, or both. Add a dash of grenadine and garnish with a maraschino cherry.

The Food

STICKS, SKEWERS AND MEATY TREATS

AN ANTIPASTI PLATTER

Ah, the antipasti platter – *grazie mille, Italia*! This is probably **the perfect way to eat while you're drinking and ideal for a party**. A little bit of ham, a little bit of cheese, olives, artichoke hearts – it's perfect, it's simple, it's low maintenance when it seems high maintenance. In short, it's effortless, like classic Italian style. (Let's face it, a perfectly sliced sliver of *prosciutto di Parma* is just as elegant as a perfectly cut Pucci dress...)

There aren't any real rules to assembling a good platter of antipasti – just add lots of what you like. I suggest you hop on your Vespa (or the number 22 bus) and head to an Italian deli to pick up a few things. I like to include 4–6 of the following:

SALAMI:

There are so many types, from all across Italy. Among my favourites are:
- *Milano*: finely chopped, smooth, mildly peppery pork-based sausage.
- *Calabrese*: spicy and fatty – just gorgeous.
- *Finocchiona*: in a thick white casing, this salami is full of fennel. It must be sliced very thinly – if you manage to get a whole one, ask your local deli to slice it for you.

PROSCIUTTO CRUDO:

Dry cured ham that is made using the hind legs of heritage-breed pigs, which are salted and then hung. The most famous are *prosciutto di Parma* and *prosciutto di San Daniele*. They are both excellent, though the San Daniele has a sweeter flavour because less salt is used in the curing process.

PROSCIUTTO COTTO:

Simple boiled ham, sometimes flavoured with herbs and spices.

MORTADELLA:

Smoked sausage from Bologna – this is where the American term "baloney" comes from. It is very smoothly minced pork and beef, dotted with pieces of pork fat. To be a real mortadella, the sausage must contain 15 per cent pork fat.

BRESAOLA:

Hailing from Lombardy, this is dark ruby-red salted and air-dried beef. Delicious with rocket, Parmesan and lemon juice.

GORGONZOLA CHEESE:

Made from full-fat cows' milk in Lombardy and Piedmont, this is a blue-veined cheese with a crumbly texture and a sharp taste. Great with a handful of walnuts.

TALEGGIO:

I always have a chunk of this funky, stinky cows' milk cheese from Lombardy ready to smear on bread. Someone once said there is something almost "beefy" about its flavour – and I agree.

PECORINO ROMANO:

Salty, sharp sheep's milk cheese from Lazio and Sardinia, with a long history. Ancient scribes from Pliny the Elder to Hippocrates raved about the stuff, and it was a staple of the Roman soldier's diet. I love it with a Negroni (see page 24) – something about its saltiness makes it a perfect pairing.

MOZZARELLA DI BUFALA:

Probably the most famous Italian cheese after Parmesan. I must say, I'd usually serve this separately with some figs or perfectly ripe tomatoes, basil and good olive oil, but it's up to you...

PEARS DRIZZLED WITH HONEY:

On the first night of our honeymoon in Rome, the restaurant was closed (well, it was Sunday, but still, HORRORS!). The bartender kindly served us this along with a selection of cheeses. I was smitten. And given the honey, I suppose it was rather apt.

FIGS OR PLUMS:

One rule, and one rule only: they must be *ripe*.

BREAD:

A good crusty loaf of your choosing.

OLIVES:

Choose your favourites – mine are French: Picholines. Just perfect! But taste the different types and pick your own olive hero.

ARTICHOKE HEARTS:

These usually come from a jar or a can. Try to find the roasted ones, and serve with a drizzle of extra virgin olive oil and some parsley.

ROASTED RED PEPPERS

You could buy these ready roasted in a jar, but they are so easy to make.

MAKES 8–12

4 red peppers

3 tablespoons extra virgin olive oil

sea salt flakes and freshly ground black pepper

Holding them with tongs, one at a time, place the peppers over the gas flame of your hob. Turn them a few times until they are completely charred and blackened. If you don't cook on gas, you can also char them under a hot grill. Place the peppers in a bowl and cover with clingfilm, or put them in a plastic bag and seal. Leave for about 30 minutes – the steam will make them easier to peel. When they are cool, peel them gently and cut into strips, removing the seeds and stalks. Toss in the olive oil and season with salt and pepper.

THINGS ON STICKS

Everyone loves food on sticks, wrapped in bacon or not. Frankly, I think half the fun of planning a party is the chance to create some new combinations and serve some old classics (honey-glazed sausage, anyone? See page 76). Here are a few of my current favourite things on sticks. They are fairly free-form – each idea is for one stick – *just make as many as you need*.

EACH RECIPE MAKES 1

1. FETA, WATERMELON AND MINT

1 mint leaf

1 cube of ripe watermelon

1 cube of good-quality Greek feta cheese

2. ROASTED VEGETABLE MEDLEY

2 slices of roasted carrot

1 slice of roasted baby aubergine

1 piece of Roasted Red Pepper (see page 61)

1 slice of roasted courgette

...all drizzled with some reduced balsamic vinegar

1.   2.

Quails' Eggs with Cumin
Salt and Black Pepper
PAGE 87

3.
FIG,
BOCCONCINI,
HAM AND BASIL

¼ ripe fig

1 basil leaf

1 strip of prosciutto ham

1 small bocconcini or cube
of mozzarella cheese

4.
SMOKY
THE DUCK

¼ pickled walnut

1 small slice of
smoked duck

5.
CONQUISTADOR
ON HORSEBACK

1 slice of bottled
piquillo pepper

1 small slice of Serrano ham

1 cube of Manchego cheese

GRAPES, STILTON AND FIGS

I really don't think recipes come much easier than this…but the combination is **a perfect balance of sweet, sharp and salty.** *Canapé heaven*.

MAKES 24

24 green seedless grapes

150g (5½oz) Stilton cheese, cut into 24 cubes

6 small dried figs, quartered

With a cocktail stick, skewer first a grape, then a cube of Stilton and then a fig quarter. Repeat to make 24 sticks. If you have longer sticks, just double the ingredients on each one. It makes for one gorgeous mouthful.

JERK CHICKEN POPPADUMS
WITH MANGO SALSA

A little mouthful of Caribbean sunshine. *Beware: they have a bite!*

MAKES 26–30

250g (9oz) boneless, skinless chicken thighs or breasts

1–2 tablespoons good-quality jerk marinade

a squeeze of lime juice

26–30 mini poppadums

For the Mango Salsa

100g (3½oz) ripe mango, chopped

½ small red onion, finely chopped

1 tablespoon chopped coriander

1 red chilli, deseeded and chopped (optional)

juice of ½ lime

a pinch of sea salt flakes

Place the chicken pieces in a large non-reactive bowl and add the jerk marinade and lime juice. Cover and leave to marinate in the fridge for about an hour.

Preheat the oven to 180°C (350°F), Gas Mark 4. Transfer the chicken to a roasting tray and bake for 20–25 minutes, or until cooked through. Leave to cool.

Meanwhile, to make the salsa, gently mix all the ingredients together in a non-reactive bowl and set aside.

Arrange the poppadums on a serving plate. Cut the chicken into 1cm (½-inch) dice and pile a little on to each poppadum. Top each with some mango salsa and serve promptly.

Kay's Tip...

I favour the Walkerswood brand of jerk marinade – it's spiky and fiery, and contrasts beautifully with the sweetness of the mango. There are so many brands out there that I advise you to taste your marinade before using. You can then judge its heat level and add a dash of hot sauce, if you like. It will also help you decide whether or not to use chilli in the salsa.

STICKY SPICED CHICKEN WINGS
WITH THAI PEANUT BRITTLE DIPPING SAUCE

These are always **a real favourite, sticky and sweet** with a good punch of pepper and coriander. The executive assistant manager at the charming Tamarind Village Hotel in Chiang Mai, Khun Jao Fa, introduced me to the fabulous dipping sauce. I've cut back on the chilli and added some fresh coriander to soften and brighten it a little – but beware, it is still a spicy little dip! *Just make sure you've plenty of napkins to go round* – there will be a lot of dirty fingers.

MAKES 40 PIECES

20 chicken wings

1 tablespoon vegetable oil

2 tablespoons thick soy sauce or kecap manis

2 tablespoons light soy sauce

2 tablespoons caster sugar

4–6 garlic cloves, finely chopped

½ tablespoon coriander seeds, crushed

a dash of Thai fish sauce (nam pla) (optional)

freshly ground white pepper

For the Thai Peanut Brittle Dipping Sauce

6 coriander roots, cut into chunks

6–8 garlic cloves, peeled

4–6 bird's eye chillies

170g (6oz) peanut brittle, broken into pieces

4 tablespoons Thai fish sauce (nam pla)

4 tablespoons fresh lime juice

2 teaspoons sugar

4 tablespoons warm water

2 tablespoons chopped coriander

Cut the chicken wings into their 3 separate joints and discard the tips or save them to make stock. Place the remaining 40 pieces in a large bowl. Place all the remaining ingredients, except those for the sauce, in a separate bowl and mix together. Pour the mixture over the chicken and toss thoroughly to coat. Cover and leave to marinate in the fridge for at least an hour.

Meanwhile, make the dipping sauce. Using a pestle and mortar, bash and grind the coriander root, garlic and chillies to a smooth paste. Add the peanut brittle and grind to a coarse mixture, mixing the brittle with the other ingredients as you go. Add the fish sauce, lime juice, sugar and measured water and stir them into the sauce. Finally, stir in the chopped coriander. If the sauce is too thick, add a little more water. Transfer to a small bowl and set aside.

When you're ready to cook, preheat the oven to 200°C (400°F), Gas Mark 6. Place the chicken pieces on a baking sheet and bake for about 30 minutes, turning once, until cooked through. They should be sticky and delicious. Serve with the dipping sauce.

Kay's Tip...

If you would like to tone down the spice in the dipping sauce even further, deseed the chillies before you pound them into the paste.

CHICKEN WINGS

WITH BASQUE-STYLE "KETCHUP"

In Spain, most people bake these chicken wings or even thighs smothered in this delicious "ketchup", known to the Spanish as *mojo rojo*. Mine is a deconstructed version because **I prefer the contrast of the chicken's salty, crispy texture with the sweetness and gentle heat of the sauce**. The *mojo rojo* can be used with eggs or fish, and is particularly good in a morning-after bacon sandwich, especially if you've enjoyed a few too many cocktails the night before.

SERVES 4–6

125ml (4fl oz) olive oil

8–10 chicken wings, jointed
(see page 67)

For the Mojo Rojo

2 tablespoons olive oil

1 large onion, chopped

300g (10½oz) red and orange
peppers (about 1 of each), cored,
deseeded and sliced into strips

2 garlic cloves, chopped

3 tomatoes, skinned, deseeded
and chopped

1–2 tablespoons sherry vinegar

1 tablespoon sugar

1 teaspoon piment d'espelette,
plus extra to serve (optional)

sea salt flakes and freshly ground
black pepper

First, make the *mojo rojo*. In a medium-sized saucepan, heat the oil, then add the onion and peppers and cook for a few minutes. Add the garlic and tomatoes. Season with a pinch of salt and cook gently until soft and beginning to break down – about 3–5 minutes. Turn down the heat, add the vinegar and sugar and cook until syrupy. You might need to add a splash of water here if it seems too thick. Allow to cool slightly before transferring to a blender or food processor. Season with black pepper and the *piment d'espelette*, then blend until smooth. Taste and adjust the seasoning, then set aside until needed.

In a sturdy frying pan, heat the 125ml (4fl oz) oil over a medium heat. Season the chicken pieces with salt, then add to the pan and cook until crispy and golden brown – about 15–20 minutes. Stab the thickest piece with a skewer to make sure they are cooked through – the juices should run clear – then set aside on kitchen paper. Sprinkle with some extra salt.

Serve the wings with some of the *mojo rojo* drizzled over them and some extra *piment d'espelette* sprinkled over the top, if you like. Serve the rest of the *mojo rojo* in a bowl on the side.

Kay's Tip...

I love the soft warmth of *piment d'espelette*, the star chilli of the Basque country. You can buy it powdered in small jars.

MINI LAARP LETTUCE ROLLS

Spicy, tart and fragrant, these canapés are the perfect appetite-sharpener to have with drinks before dinner.

MAKES 24–30

500g (1lb 2oz) boneless, skinless lean duck, finely chopped or minced

2 tablespoons Thai fish sauce (nam pla)

3 tablespoons fresh lime juice

½–1 teaspoon roasted chilli powder

4 Thai shallots or 2 regular shallots, thinly sliced

1–2 tablespoons ground toasted rice (see Kay's Tip)

a large handful of mint leaves, torn

1 lemon grass stalk, tough outer leaves removed, core thinly sliced (optional)

24–30 Baby Gem lettuce leaves

lime wedges, to serve

Bring a saucepan of water to the boil over a medium heat and add the duck. Bring back to the boil, and cook the duck to your liking: it will take just a minute or so for it to be pink, a bit longer if you want it done through.

Transfer the duck to a large bowl and add the fish sauce, lime juice, chilli powder, shallots, ground rice, mint and lemon grass, if using. Mix well.

Line a plate with Baby Gem lettuce leaves, spoon the laarp inside them and serve with lime wedges while still warm, if possible.

Kay's Tip...

You can buy ground toasted rice in Asian supermarkets or make your own. To make your own, take a large handful of uncooked sticky rice (or normal Thai jasmine rice, if necessary) and place it in a dry wok or frying pan over a low heat. Toast the rice, moving it all the time, until it smells nutty and has turned a dark golden brown. Grind it in a spice or coffee grinder, or with a pestle and mortar. Store in a jar and use as required.

SPICY SCOTCH QUAILS' EGGS
WITH SAFFRON AIOLI

We all have memories of Scotch eggs, some good, some bad. I've been served some shockers in my time. But when they're done right, they're sublime. These mini versions, made with creamy yolked quails' eggs, are **perfectly canapé-sized** and, if I do say so myself, *very, very good*. You can either make the aioli from scratch or follow my tip opposite to make a cheat's version.

MAKES 24–32

For the Scotch Eggs

400g (14oz) sausagemeat

100g (3½oz) 'nduja sausage, skinned if in casing

1 tablespoon chopped flat leaf parsley

vegetable oil, for deep-frying

24–32 quails' eggs, hard-boiled, cooled and shelled (see page 87)

100g (3½oz) plain flour

1 egg, lightly beaten

125g (4½oz) dried breadcrumbs

sea salt flakes and freshly ground black pepper

To make the Scotch eggs, combine the sausagemeat, 'nduja and parsley in a large bowl. Season with salt and pepper. Heat a little oil in a frying pan and fry off 1 teaspoon of the sausage mixture until just cooked. Taste, and adjust the seasoning if necessary.

Line 2 baking sheets with nonstick baking paper. Divide the sausage mixture into 24–32 pieces, then flatten into discs and place a quail's egg on each disc. Roll the sausagemeat around the egg so that it is completely enclosed and as smooth as you can get it. Pop them on to the lined baking sheets and refrigerate for 10–15 minutes.

Meanwhile, in a deep-fat fryer or deep saucepan, heat the oil to 180°C (350°F), or until a cube of bread turns golden in 30 seconds. Roll each of the Scotch eggs in the flour, then in the beaten egg and finally in the breadcrumbs. Gently deep-fry the eggs, a few at a time, for 3–4 minutes until crisp and golden brown. Remove and drain on kitchen paper. Serve hot with the saffron aioli.

To make the aioli, first make sure your mortar and pestle are warm and dry. Crush the garlic in the mortar with the salt, getting it as smooth as possible. Add the egg yolks, stirring and pressing, always in the same direction, until combined. When the mixture feels silky, start adding the olive oil a drop at a time, stirring and pressing constantly.

For the Aioli

2 garlic cloves, peeled

a good pinch of sea salt flakes

2 large very fresh egg yolks

250ml (9fl oz) extra virgin olive oil

½ teaspoon saffron threads (optional)

a dash of fresh lemon juice

If you are making a saffron aioli, add the saffron when the mixture seems to be holding together, then continue adding the oil gradually: the mixture will thicken and start to feel more "jellyish". At this point, you can add more of the oil, in a thin stream, continuing to stir and beat until you have a nice wobbly, creamy mayonnaise. Stir in the lemon juice to taste. It can be refrigerated, tightly covered, for up to 2 days. Serve at room temperature.

Kay's Tip...

To make a cheat's aioli, simply mix together 250g (9oz) good-quality mayonnaise, 2 crushed garlic cloves, a dash of lemon juice and, for a saffron aioli, ½ teaspoon saffron threads in a bowl. Serve at room temperature.

SKEWERS OF PORCHETTA

Porchetta or pork belly stuffed with herbs and garlic, roasted long and slow and served in bread rolls slathered with salsa verde is one of the great delights of a weekend in Florence. It is far too substantial to be called a snack. But I love those flavours. So here I have made a **daintier version that still packs a punch** and can be served on sticks, making them *perfect for cocktail parties.*

SERVES 6

1 tablespoon fennel seeds

2 rosemary sprigs, leaves only, chopped

4 tablespoons olive oil

450g (1lb) pork leg steaks, cut into bite-sized pieces

1 garlic clove, crushed in its skin, then skin discarded

1 dried peperoncino chilli (optional)

sea salt flakes and freshly ground black pepper

Salsa Verde (see page 102), to serve

Using a pestle and mortar, crush the fennel seeds and rosemary leaves together, then mix in the olive oil. Pour the mixture into a bowl, add the pork and stir to coat evenly. Cover and leave to marinate in the fridge for 1–3 hours. Season with salt and pepper.

Heat a frying pan until hot, then add the pork with all the oil marinade. Cook, tossing the pork in the pan, until golden and cooked through – about 6–8 minutes. Just before you take the pork out of the pan, add the crushed garlic and the peperoncino, if using, and stir it around – you want it to stick to the meat, but not to burn.

Serve piping hot, with sticks or little forks for each guest and some salsa verde on the side.

STICKY SAUSAGES

This is an oldie, but my God, it's good. And what's even better, **it scales up incredibly easily**. I've based this on what I can fit in a standard 35 x 25cm (14 x 10-inch) roasting tray. *Scaling up simply requires preparing a second tray*.

MAKES 40

40 good-quality cocktail sausages

2 tablespoons grainy or Dijon mustard

2 tablespoons runny honey

½ teaspoon cayenne pepper (optional)

Preheat the oven to 200°C (400°F), Gas Mark 6. Space the sausages evenly in the roasting tray. Bake for about 25 minutes, turning once.

Meanwhile, mix the mustard and honey together in a bowl. Add the cayenne pepper if you want some extra spice.

When the sausages are almost done, baste them liberally with the mustard and honey mixture. Return to the oven and bake until they are sticky and golden brown. This should take about 5–10 minutes, but keep an eye on them. You don't want them to burn.

Serve on cocktail sticks, because it's a known fact: everything tastes better on a stick. Or in a taco.

MOORISH LAMB SKEWERS

Pintxos morunos ("Moorish skewers") are now usually made with pork. But I prefer to use lamb, so that the recipe properly reflects Spain's Moorish legacy. You will need some pintxo sticks or skewers to make these; if they're wooden, give them a bit of a soak in some water for about 5 minutes to avoid them splintering on the heat.

MAKES 8–12

500g (1lb 2oz) lamb neck fillet, cut into 2–3cm (¾–1¼-inch) chunks

3 tablespoons olive oil

2 teaspoons ras el hanout

2 teaspoons cumin seeds, toasted

1 teaspoon hot smoked paprika (optional)

½ teaspoon finely grated lemon zest

1 teaspoon dried oregano

2 garlic cloves, crushed

½ teaspoon freshly ground black pepper

a pinch of sea salt flakes

chopped flat leaf parsley, to garnish

To serve

Roasted Red Peppers (see page 61)

lemon wedges

PX Drizzle (optional, see Kay's Tip)

Place the lamb chunks in a non-reactive bowl. Add the remaining ingredients, except those to garnish and serve, and stir to combine. Cover and leave to marinate in the fridge for 1–3 hours.

Heat a flat griddle pan or heavy-based frying pan until hot. While it heats up, thread the chunks of lamb on to some pintxo sticks or skewers. Season with a little more salt and pop them on to the hot surface. Cook, turning every now and then, until cooked through. It will take about 3–4 minutes on each side – you want a bit of crust on the outside and a nice pink interior.

Remove from the heat and sprinkle with chopped parsley. Serve with the Roasted Red Peppers, lemon wedges and a little PX Drizzle, if you like.

Kay's Tip...

To make a PX Drizzle for the skewers, place 200ml (7fl oz) Pedro Ximénez sherry vinegar in a saucepan. Bring to the boil, then turn down to a simmer and gently reduce until you are left with 100ml (3½fl oz). Leave to cool, then bottle until you need it.

LAMB CUTLETS
WITH MINT AND CAPER AIOLI

Little lamb cutlets, French trimmed, provide a **nature-made bone handle** for your finger food. *I have added an English twist to the aioli by adding mint and capers*.

MAKES 12

12 lamb cutlets

1 garlic clove, halved

olive oil, for rubbing

sea salt flakes and freshly ground black pepper

For the Mint and Caper Aioli

1 quantity of Aioli (see page 73)

a large handful of mint leaves, chopped

1 teaspoon Moscatel vinegar (or other wine vinegar)

2–3 tablespoons capers, rinsed and drained

Rub the lamb cutlets on both sides with the halved garlic clove, then rub them with olive oil on both sides and season well with salt and pepper. Set aside.

In a blender or food processor, blend the aioli with the mint and vinegar. Scrape into a bowl and stir in the capers.

Heat a flat griddle pan or frying pan until very hot, then cook the lamb for about 2–3 minutes on each side until the cutlets are well browned but still nicely pink inside.

Serve on a platter with some of the aioli drizzled over and the remainder on the side.

LIGHTLY SPICED FILLET OF BEEF
WITH GRIDDLED RED PEPPERS

You could use sirloin for this, but I love the butteriness of the fillet steak against the smoky paprika and sweet red peppers. For a change, you could also cut the steak into large chunks before popping on to its skewers.

MAKES 8–12 SKEWERS

500g (1lb 2oz) fillet steak, about 2.5–3cm (1–1¼ inches) thick

2 long red peppers, halved lengthways, cored and deseeded, then halved again across the middle

For the marinade

2 tablespoons olive oil, plus extra for coating

1 teaspoon mild smoked paprika

a good pinch of dried oregano

1 garlic clove, crushed

sea salt flakes and freshly ground black pepper

Mix all the marinade ingredients together in a bowl. Slice the steak into lengthways strips about 1cm (½ inch) thick. Pop them into the marinade, cover and leave in the fridge for about an hour.

Meanwhile, heat a flat griddle pan or frying pan until very hot. Coat the red pepper halves in olive oil and place in the hot pan. Season with a little salt. Turn them every now and then. Add a splash of cold water – the steam will help them soften. Then, when they are soft and have caught some colour, remove and set aside.

Now take the skewers and thread a beef slice on to each one – you want the skewer to pierce the meat 3 times. Cook until you have a nice char on the outside, but the meat is still pink and tender on the inside. This should take about 2 minutes.

Remove from the heat and serve with the red peppers.

CURED BEEF WRAPPED AROUND SPEARS OF ROASTED ASPARAGUS

This plate of food combines two of my absolute favourite things – and it's **such a doddle to make** that you can spend more time sipping and chatting with pals, which, after all, is *what a party is all about.*

MAKES 18–24

18–24 spears of asparagus, washed and trimmed

3–4 thyme sprigs

2 garlic cloves, bashed in their skins

2 tablespoons olive oil

18–24 slices of bresaola

sea salt flakes and freshly ground black pepper

Preheat the oven to 200°C (400°F), Gas Mark 6.

Dry the asparagus thoroughly. Place it in a roasting tray with the thyme, garlic and olive oil. Season with salt and pepper and toss until everything is well combined.

Pop the tray into the oven, giving it a gentle shake now and then, for 15–20 minutes, or until the asparagus is cooked through but still firm. Remove from the oven and leave to cool slightly.

When cool enough to handle, wrap a slice of bresaola around each spear and serve.

BEEF CARPACCIO
WITH PARMESAN CRISPS AND ROCKET

Crisp, salty, sharp discs of cheese with a pile of rare beef nestled on top and capped off with a punchy horseradish cream – **these little bites are perfect foils** to the drier drinks: *a Martini, a glass of Champagne…*

MAKES ABOUT 24

250g (9oz) piece of fillet steak

1 tablespoon olive oil

a good handful of rocket

sea salt flakes and freshly ground black pepper

lemon wedges, to serve

For the Parmesan Crisps

125g (4½oz) Parmesan cheese

finely grated zest of 1 lemon

1–2 teaspoons thyme leaves

For the Horseradish Cream

2 teaspoons grated horseradish

4 teaspoons soured cream

a squeeze of lemon juice

To make the Parmesan crisps, preheat the oven to 180°C (350°F), Gas Mark 4, and line a baking sheet with a silicone liner or nonstick baking paper. If you only have greaseproof paper, make sure you grease it.

Grate the Parmesan into a bowl, then add the lemon zest and thyme, season with black pepper and mix gently until well combined. Place a 6.5cm (2½-inch) round pastry cutter on the lined baking sheet and sprinkle a heaped tablespoonful of the cheese mixture into it. Even out the cheese, but don't flatten it entirely. Repeat to make 24 rounds, spacing them apart on the baking sheet.

Bake for 4–6 minutes until golden and melted. Be careful not to burn them. Transfer the Parmesan crisps to a wire rack to cool and set aside until needed, or store in an airtight container overnight.

To cook the beef, heat a flat griddle pan or frying pan over a high heat. Rub both sides of the steak with the olive oil, then season it thoroughly with salt and pepper. Cook the steak in the hot pan for 2–3 minutes on each side until seared on the outside but still rare inside. Transfer to a plate and leave to rest for 10–15 minutes, then refrigerate until completely cold. This will make the beef easier to slice.

To make the horseradish cream, place all the ingredients in a small bowl, season with salt and pepper and mix together thoroughly.

To assemble the canapés, slice the steak very thinly. Place a rolled-up slice on top of each Parmesan crisp and top with a little horseradish cream and a couple of leaves of rocket. Serve with lemon wedges.

QUAILS' EGGS
WITH CUMIN SALT AND BLACK PEPPER

Sophisticated but oh, so simple! The secret is to get the eggs just so – you want a little glossy "give" in the yolk, but for the white to be firm. *Enlist help with the shelling over a glass of something cool...*

MAKES 24

24 quails' eggs

sea salt flakes

1 teaspoon freshly ground black pepper

1 teaspoon ground cumin

Check the eggs over and discard any that are broken or cracked. Bring a saucepan of salted water to a rolling boil. Gently lower the eggs into the water – I use a slotted spoon – and boil them for 2½–3 minutes. You may need to do this in 2 or 3 batches to avoid overcrowding the pan, which will lower the water temperature too much and affect cooking.

Remove the eggs from the pan and plunge immediately into a large bowl of ice-cold water. Leave to cool completely, then carefully shell them. Mix 2 tablespoons salt, the pepper and cumin together and serve in little piles alongside the eggs. If you have any cumin salt left over, keep it in a container and use it as a condiment – it's delicious.

See a picture of this dish

PAGE 35

EACH RECIPE MAKES 24

DEVILLED EGGS THREE WAYS

I do love a cheeky devilled egg – **how much more retro can you get?** It's a classic of this oeuvre (ouch!). I used to make dozens of these with my mum's great friend Shirley when she threw her annual Christmas extravaganza. The first recipe is fairly classic, while the second is an updated version: smoked salmon and dill. The final recipe is rather more left field, but the sour-hot Korean flavours set off the salty crisp Spanish ham and almonds. *They're all pretty darned good and devilish indeed!*

CLASSIC

12 eggs, hard-boiled, cooled and shelled

4–6 tablespoons Aioli (see page 73)

1–2 teaspoons hot smoked paprika, plus extra to garnish

1–2 teaspoons Moscatel vinegar (or other wine vinegar)

1 tablespoon finely chopped chives, plus extra to garnish

24 small cooked peeled prawns

sea salt flakes and freshly ground black pepper

Carefully cut the eggs in half along their lengths and scoop the yolks into a bowl. Arrange the whites on a serving plate.

Add the aioli, paprika and vinegar to the yolks and mash well. Season with salt and pepper and gently stir in the chives. Taste and adjust the seasoning. Carefully scoop the yolk mixture back into the whites and top each egg with a prawn. Sprinkle with extra chopped chives and paprika before serving.

SMOKED SALMON AND DILL

12 eggs, hard-boiled, cooled and shelled

4 tablespoons soured cream

3 teaspoons English mustard

1 teaspoon grated horseradish

1 tablespoon fresh lemon juice

1 tablespoon finely chopped dill, plus extra
to garnish

25–30g (about 1oz) smoked salmon,
cut into 24 pieces

sea salt flakes and freshly ground black pepper

Carefully cut the eggs in half along their lengths
and scoop the yolks into a large bowl. Arrange the
whites on a serving plate.

Add the soured cream, mustard, horseradish and
lemon juice to the yolks and mash well together.
Season with salt and plenty of pepper, then gently
stir through the chopped dill. Taste and adjust the
seasoning, if necessary, and if you feel it's a little
dry, add a dash more soured cream.

Scoop or pipe the yolk mixture back into the
whites and top with the slivers of smoked salmon.
Sprinkle with a little more dill and a grinding of
black pepper before serving.

K-POP PLAYS SEVILLE

4–6 slices of Serrano ham

a handful of Marcona almonds

12 eggs, hard-boiled, cooled and shelled

4–6 tablespoons Gochujang Aioli (see Kay's Tip)

a dash of lemon juice or vinegar (optional)

1 tablespoon finely chopped chives, to garnish

First, make the Serrano ham and almond garnish. Preheat the oven to 180°C (350°F), Gas Mark 4. Lay the ham slices on a piece of foil. Fold it over the ham, then sandwich it tightly between 2 baking sheets. Pop into the oven for about 15 minutes. Remove the ham from the sheets and the foil and set aside on kitchen paper to drain and cool. When cold, it can be kept in an airtight container until needed.

Turn the oven down to 150°C (300°F), Gas Mark 2. Spread the almonds out on a baking sheet and toast for 10–15 minutes, or until just crisped up. Remove from the oven and, when cool enough to handle, smash them up a bit. Once completely cooled, set aside in an airtight container until needed.

Carefully cut the eggs in half along their lengths and scoop the yolks into a bowl. Arrange the whites on a serving plate. Add the gochujang aioli to the yolks and mash well together. Taste and adjust the seasoning – you might want to add a dash of lemon juice or vinegar. Scoop the mixture back into the whites. Top each egg half with a sliver of crisped ham and a sprinkle of toasted almonds. Sprinkle with the chives before serving.

Kay's Tip...

Gochujang paste is a fermented Korean chilli paste that packs a punch. It's a great storecupboard staple. To make Gochujang Aioli, follow the Aioli recipe on page 73, then stir in 2 tablespoons gochujang paste (more if you really like it fiery).

SOUPS, CHIPS, DIPS AND DIPPERS

THREE SOUP SHOTS

The great thing about these savoury cocktails is that **you can make them well ahead of time**, and *serve hot or cold when guests arrive*. You may want to serve these with little spoons.

GREEN GAZPACHO WITH SERRANO HAM CRISPS

MAKES 24–28 SHOTS

300g (10½oz) cucumber, peeled and roughly chopped

1 green pepper, cored, deseeded and roughly chopped

2 garlic cloves, chopped

4 spring onions, roughly chopped

100g (3½oz) baby spinach

125g (4½oz) frozen peas

a good handful of mint leaves

a good handful of basil leaves

25g (1oz) blanched almonds

2 slices of white bread, toasted and roughly torn

juice of ½ lemon

1 tablespoon sherry vinegar

sea salt flakes and freshly ground black pepper

4–6 slices of Serrano ham, fried until crisp, to garnish

Bright green and fresh as a summer's day, this soup should be served icy cold in small shot glasses.

Pop 5–6 ice cubes into a blender or food processor and blend to crush them, then add the remaining ingredients, in batches if necessary, and blend until smooth. Season with salt and pepper. Make sure the soup isn't *too* thick – you want guests to be able to sip it easily – so add a dash of cold water to loosen, if necessary.

Break each of the ham slices into 4–6 pieces. Pour the soup into shot glasses and garnish each with a shard of crisp Serrano ham.

ROASTED BEETROOT, APPLE AND HORSERADISH SOUP

The brilliant Schiaparelli pink of this soup is reason enough to make it – it also tastes absolutely sublime.

MAKES 24–30 SHOTS

500g (1lb 2oz) beetroot, chopped into even chunks

250g (9oz) Cox's apples, quartered and cored

3 thyme sprigs

1 rosemary sprig

4 tablespoons olive oil

1 onion, finely chopped

1 garlic clove, chopped

1 litre (1¾ pints) vegetable stock

2 teaspoons grated horseradish

a pinch of sugar

sea salt flakes and freshly ground black pepper

soured cream, to garnish (optional)

Preheat the oven to 200°C (400°F), Gas Mark 6. Place the beetroot and apples in a roasting tray with the thyme and rosemary. Drizzle with half the olive oil and season with a little salt and pepper, then cover with foil. Bake for 40 minutes until the beetroot chunks are soft. Set aside, still covered, to cool. This will help them retain their moisture and make them easier to peel. Peel the cooled beetroot and apples and set aside.

Heat the remaining olive oil in a large saucepan over a medium heat, add the onion and cook until soft and lightly golden. Add the garlic and stir for another minute or so. Add the beetroot and apples and stir well. Pour in the vegetable stock and bring to the boil, then turn down the heat and simmer for 5–10 minutes.

Add the horseradish and sugar and season with salt and pepper. Remove from the heat and leave the soup to cool for a few minutes. Transfer to a blender or food processor and blend until smooth. Taste and adjust the seasoning, if necessary.

Serve warm or cold, garnished with a tiny swirl of soured cream, if you like.

TOMATO AND BASIL SOUP
WITH GRILLED CHEESE SANDWICHES

Before I say anything else, I will plead with you to make this soup only when you can get ripe, lush tomatoes: it will make such a difference to the taste and the colour. The little grilled cheese sandwiches on the side are a winner every time!

MAKES 24–28 SHOTS

500g (1lb 2oz) tomatoes

1 tablespoon olive oil

½ onion, chopped

2 garlic cloves, chopped

750ml (1¼ pints) vegetable stock

1–2 tablespoons tomato purée (in case your tomatoes are not the best)

a large handful of basil leaves, torn

sea salt flakes and freshly ground black pepper

For the Grilled Cheese Sandwiches

a little butter

8 slices of white bread

enough sliced cheese for 4 rounds of sandwiches

Place the tomatoes in a heatproof bowl and pour over boiling water to cover. Leave for 1–2 minutes, then drain and slip off their skins. Deseed the tomatoes, then roughly chop.

Heat the oil in a large saucepan over a low heat, add the onion and sweat gently until soft. Add the garlic and cook for another 1–2 minutes. Add the tomatoes and stir well, then add the stock and tomato purée and bring to the boil. Turn down the heat and simmer for 5–10 minutes, then season with salt and pepper.

Remove from the heat and leave to cool for a few minutes. Transfer to a blender or food processor and blend until smooth. Add the basil and blend again until smooth. Taste and adjust the seasoning, if necessary. Remove from the heat and set aside.

To make the grilled cheese sandwiches, butter the slices of white bread and make into 4 rounds of sandwiches filled with the sliced cheese, buttered sides out. Cook in a hot, dry frying pan until golden on both sides, then cut into mini sandwiches.

Serve the soup warm or cold, with the little sandwiches on the side, or on sticks if you like.

Kay's Tip...

Make sure you don't serve the soup shots too hot: people may burn themselves by knocking it back and it will be hard to hold. Also make sure you have heatproof glasses!

MUM'S RETRO DIP

This wasn't retro when Mum made it back in the 1970s, obviously – but it is deliciously so now. There was never an official recipe for it as such; we just chucked in whatever we fancied. But the Publisher expects, so here is a more regimented version. Once you've made it, **feel free to ad lib as you please.** Add blue cheese, soured cream, finely chopped peppers: make it yours. *And have fun. It is a party, after all.*

MAKES 600G (1LB 5OZ)

460g (1lb) cream cheese

2 teaspoons Worcestershire sauce

2 teaspoons Tabasco sauce

juice of 1 lime

3 spring onions, very finely chopped

½ large red chilli, deseeded and chopped, plus extra to garnish

1–2 tablespoons chopped chives, plus extra to garnish

a handful of coriander and/or basil, finely chopped

1 tablespoon milk, if needed

sea salt flakes and freshly ground black pepper

crudités, to serve

Place the cream cheese in a large bowl and beat until smooth and creamy. Add the Worcestershire sauce, Tabasco and lime juice, stirring well to combine. Feel free to add more Tabasco if you want to make the dip spicier.

Add the spring onions, chilli and herbs, mixing well to combine. If the dip seems a little stiff, add the milk. Season with salt and pepper, then taste and adjust the seasoning to your liking.

Garnish with extra chives and chilli, and serve with a good selection of crudités.

Kay's Tip...

You can also serve this with crisps or breadsticks, if you'd rather.

LOU CACHAT

Let's face it, this is not so much a recipe as **a Provençal tradition** – a way of using up leftover cheese, all chopped up and squished together. Pungent but perfect, *this is at its best after a day in the fridge.*

SERVES 8–12

3 garlic cloves, peeled

400–500g (14oz–1lb 2oz) leftover soft cheese (goats' and sheep's cheeses are particularly good)

a good pinch of thyme leaves

1 rosemary sprig, leaves only

2 tablespoons eau de vie, brandy or Calvados

sea salt flakes and freshly ground black pepper

chunks of baguette, to serve

Using a pestle and mortar, crush the garlic with a few sea salt flakes to form a smooth paste. Add the cheeses and mash them together. Add the herbs, alcohol and some pepper, then blend together until smooth. You may find a large fork or potato masher handy. Put the mixture into a jam jar or Mason jar, cover and refrigerate until needed.

Take the Lou Cachat out of the fridge at least 30 minutes before you want to serve it, then serve it in its jar with chunks of baguette.

TAPENADE

Laden with Provençal flavours, this garlicky tapenade should be used sparingly! Serve with crudités, fresh bread or crisp slices of baguette that you have toasted in the oven. Any leftovers are *delicious smothered on lamb before roasting or barbecuing*.

MAKES ABOUT 300G (10½ OUNCES)

300g (10½oz) pitted black olives

6 tablespoons capers, rinsed and drained

1 large rosemary sprig, leaves only

8 garlic cloves, chopped

6–8 tablespoons olive oil

50g (1¾oz) canned anchovy fillets in olive oil, drained (optional)

1 tablespoon brandy

juice of ½ lemon

sea salt flakes and freshly ground black pepper

Place all the ingredients in a blender or food processor and blend until well combined but still retaining some texture. Taste and add more lemon juice or adjust the seasoning if necessary.

Serve immediately, or keep tightly covered in the fridge until needed. It will keep for up to a week.

DIPS

TOMATO AND BASIL DIP

SERVES 8–12

1 tablespoon olive oil

1 onion, finely chopped

2 garlic cloves, chopped

400g (14oz) can chopped tomatoes

1 tablespoon tomato purée

1 teaspoon dried oregano

a handful of basil leaves, torn into small pieces

sea salt flakes and freshly ground black pepper

Heat the olive oil in a saucepan over a medium heat, add the onion and cook until soft. Add the garlic and cook for another couple of minutes or so, then add the tomatoes. Stir in the tomato purée and oregano, and season with salt and pepper. Cook until the sauce is thick and reduced.

Stir in the basil, then leave to cool completely before serving.

SALSA VERDE – HERBY GREEN SAUCE

SERVES 8–12

12 garlic cloves

2 x 55g (2oz) can anchovy fillets, drained

4 tablespoons capers, rinsed and drained

two large handfuls of basil

two large handfuls of mint

two large handfuls of flat leaf parsley

juice of 2 lemons

a couple of good dashes of white wine vinegar

240ml olive oil, maybe more

freshly ground black pepper

Pop all the salsa verde ingredients into a food processor or mini chopper. Whizz them up, trying to retain a little texture. Taste and adjust the seasoning, if necessary.

QUICK HUMMUS

Garlicky, lemony hummus is always a hit.

SERVES 12

2 x 400g (14oz) cans chickpeas, rinsed and drained

2 tablespoons tahini

2 garlic cloves, chopped

a good pinch of ground cumin

2 tablespoons fresh lemon juice

a good splash of extra virgin olive oil, plus extra to garnish

150–200ml (5–7fl oz) warm water

sea salt flakes and freshly ground black pepper

To garnish

a pinch of cayenne pepper or ground sumac

deep-fried garlic slices (optional)

Place the chickpeas, tahini, garlic, cumin, lemon juice and olive oil in a blender or food processor and blend until smooth. Add enough of the warm water, a little at a time, to give the hummus a smooth consistency. Season with salt and pepper.

Scoop it into a bowl and serve at room temperature, garnished with a sprinkling of cayenne pepper or sumac, a drizzle of olive oil and some fried garlic slices, if you like.

CHIPOTLE MAYONNAISE

SERVES 8–12

1 chipotle chilli in adobo sauce

3 heaped tablespoons good-quality mayonnaise

a dash of fresh lemon juice

Purée the chipotle chilli and a little sauce from the jar using a hand-held blender. Mix 2 teaspoons of the paste with the mayonnaise and lemon juice. Serve with the Crab Cakes on page 130.

TUSCAN BEAN DIP

Super-quick and easy, this can be made from pretty much what is in your cupboards and fridge. I always tend to have a few cans of beans lurking in my kitchen.

MAKES ABOUT 800G (1LB 12OZ)

2 x 400g (14oz) cans cannellini beans, rinsed and drained

2 tablespoons extra virgin olive oil

1 shallot, chopped

2 garlic cloves, chopped

1 rosemary sprig, leaves only, finely chopped

a handful of flat leaf parsley, finely chopped

150ml (5fl oz) good-quality chicken stock

sea salt flakes and freshly ground black pepper

crudités and crusty bread or breadsticks, to serve

Pop everything bar the stock into a blender or food processor. Whizz up and add the chicken stock as you're whizzing – you may not need all of it. You want a nice creamy consistency. Add salt and pepper to taste.

Serve with your choice of crudités and crusty bread or breadsticks.

PUGLIAN TARALLI BISCUITS

While *aperitivo* – the Italian concept of a well-made drink with a satisfying snack and lashings of *un certo non so che* – is very much a northern concept, it doesn't mean that they don't make **delicious drinking snacks** in the south. For example, *taralli*, which I first discovered on my honeymoon, when we stayed at the beautiful Masseria Il Frantoio, run by Signor e Signora Ballastrazzi. (La Signora is one of the most extraordinary cooks I've ever met, cooking amazing 14-course banquets for the guests, and with a deep knowledge of Puglia's culinary history.) Every evening, before heading out for dinner, we'd enjoy a glass or two of white wine in the sun-dappled courtyard, served with fat green olives and La Signora's *taralli*. This recipe isn't hers exactly, but *it's based on how she told me to make them*.

MAKES ABOUT 18–22

250g (9oz) "00" flour, plus extra for dusting

a good pinch of salt

75ml (2½fl oz) extra virgin olive oil

100ml (3½fl oz) white wine

1½ teaspoons fennel seeds

Mix together the flour and salt in a bowl and add the liquids. Bring everything together into a dough, then turn out on to a floured surface and knead for 5 minutes. Add the fennel seeds, and knead again to spread them evenly through the dough. Return the dough to a clean bowl and set aside to rest for 30 minutes or so, covered with a cloth.

When you're ready to make the *taralli*, break the dough into walnut-sized pieces, then roll each piece out into a rope that's about 4cm (1½ inches) long and 1cm (½ inch) in diameter. Shape each one into a rough circle, crossing and gently pinching the ends together.

Bring a large saucepan of water to the boil and, in batches, add the *taralli*. Cook until they float to the surface (just under a minute or so), then scoop out with a slotted spoon and set aside to dry and cool.

Preheat the oven to 190°C (375°F), Gas Mark 5. Place the *taralli* on baking sheets and bake until they are golden and crunchy – about 35 minutes. Transfer to wire racks to cool. You can store them in an airtight container until needed. They will keep for up to 3–5 days.

POLENTA "FRIES"
WITH ROSEMARY AND SEA SALT FLAKES

When I had the great pleasure of co-writing *The Tucci Table* with the ever-charming actor Stanley Tucci and his wife Felicity Blunt, this was one of the **stars of the show** – crisp, hot polenta "fries" with a herby salt. I have changed a couple of things, but otherwise, why mess with perfection? *As an alternative to the herbs in the salt, try a few shavings of truffle…*

SERVES 4–6

200g (7oz) cooked polenta, chilled

120g (4¼oz) Parmesan cheese, freshly grated

vegetable oil, for deep-frying

2 rosemary sprigs, leaves only, chopped

4 thyme sprigs, leaves only

sea salt flakes and freshly ground black pepper

Line a baking sheet with nonstick baking paper. Slice the cold polenta into finger-sized sticks, then gently roll each one in the grated Parmesan. Pop them on to the lined baking sheet and refrigerate until needed.

In a deep-fat fryer or deep saucepan, heat the oil to 180°C (350°F), or until a cube of bread turns golden in 30 seconds. Gently deep-fry the polenta sticks, in batches, for about 3–4 minutes until crisp and golden. Remove and drain on kitchen paper.

While still hot, season with salt and pepper and sprinkle with the rosemary and thyme. Serve immediately.

TAYLOR'S-STYLE
HOMEMADE POTATO CHIPS

At Taylor's Steakhouse in Los Angeles, not only do they grill up a fine T-bone ("charred and rare"), but they also make the wait enjoyable by serving warm, straight-from-the-fryer salted potato chips with one's aperitif. Keeping it classy. ***These are my homage***…

MAKES 1 BOWL

500g (1lb 2oz) potatoes

1 litre (1¾ pints) vegetable oil

a good pinch of sea salt flakes

a pinch of paprika (optional)

Peel the potatoes, then slice them very thinly, ideally with a mandoline. Soak the sliced potatoes in cold water for 10 minutes to remove the starch. Drain, then spread out on a clean tea towel to dry thoroughly.

In a deep-fat fryer or deep saucepan, heat the oil to 190°C (375°F), or until a cube of bread turns golden in 30 seconds. Gently deep-fry the chips, in batches, until they just turn golden brown. Remove immediately and drain on kitchen paper. Note that if you add too many at once, they will cool the oil and they won't cook properly.

Sprinkle the chips with the sea salt flakes and dust with the paprika, if you like.

CHEDDAR–PARMESAN BISCUITS

These delicious cheesy biscuits are **a complete doddle to make**. They're heavenly with a Dry Martini or a Champagne Cocktail – in fact with just about any cocktail. And, while they're delicious cold, these are *extra special when they're warm from the oven*.

MAKES 24

125g (4½oz) plain flour, plus extra for dusting

65g (2¼oz) cold unsalted butter, cut into cubes

30g (1oz) Cheddar cheese, grated

30g (1oz) Parmesan cheese, grated

1 large egg yolk

a large pinch of cayenne pepper, plus extra to garnish (optional)

sea salt flakes and freshly ground black pepper

Preheat the oven to 170°C (325°F), Gas Mark 3½, and line a baking sheet with nonstick baking paper. Place the flour in a large bowl and rub in the butter with your fingertips until the mixture resembles fine breadcrumbs. Stir in the grated cheeses, the egg yolk, the cayenne, a good pinch of sea salt flakes and several good grindings of black pepper. Mix well with your hands until the mixture comes together into a dough. If it seems too dry, add a splash of cold water – but just a little.

Roll out the dough on a lightly floured, cool work surface to a thickness of about 5mm (½ inch). Cut out 24 biscuits using a 5cm (2-inch) fluted pastry cutter and arrange on the lined baking sheet.

Bake for 20 minutes until lightly golden and crisp. Serve warm, straight out of the oven, if possible. Sprinkle with a little extra cayenne, if you like.

FRENCH FRY POTATOES
WITH BRAVAS SAUCE

There are so many versions of bravas sauce: some hotter than others, some sharper. They should all have a kick. This recipe makes more than you need, but it keeps in the fridge for up to a week. It is also delicious with eggs and croquettes.

SERVES 4–6

500g (1lb 2oz) King Edward or other floury potatoes, peeled and cut into 1cm (½-inch) slices, then into 1cm (½-inch) chips

vegetable oil, for deep-frying

For the Bravas Sauce
MAKES ABOUT 450ML (16FL OZ)

1 red chilli

2 tablespoons olive oil

1 small onion, finely chopped

⅓ leek, finely chopped

⅓ carrot, finely chopped

2 garlic cloves, crushed

400g (14oz) can chopped tomatoes

Soak the chips in a bowl of icy water for an hour or so.

Meanwhile, make the bravas sauce. Holding it with tongs, roast the chilli over the gas flame of your hob until its skin is blackened and blistered. If you don't cook on gas, you can also char it under a hot grill. Peel as you would a red pepper (see page 61), then deseed and chop. Heat the olive oil in a saucepan over a low heat, add the onion, leek, carrot and garlic and cook gently until soft. Add the tomatoes, tomato purée, roasted chilli, paprika, herbs and sugar and season with salt and pepper. Simmer gently for about 20 minutes until thick and reduced. Remove from the heat, add the sherry vinegar and taste and adjust the seasoning. Remove the herbs, then blitz with a hand-held blender until smooth. Leave to cool, then cover and refrigerate until needed.

Drain the chips, dry thoroughly and set aside. Heat the vegetable oil to 90°C (200°F) in a deep-fat fryer or deep saucepan. Blanch the chips for 10–15 minutes until just cooked through. You will probably have to do this in batches. Remove and drain on kitchen paper until they are completely cool, then pop them into the fridge, if you like – I find the shock of their going from being very cold straight into the very hot oil makes for extra crispiness.

When the chips are completely cold, heat the oil back up to 180°C (350°F), or until a cube of bread turns golden in 30 seconds. Gently deep-fry the chips, in batches (you don't want to lose too much

1 tablespoon tomato purée

2 teaspoons hot smoked paprika

1 bay leaf

1–2 oregano sprigs

a pinch of sugar

1–2 tablespoons sherry vinegar,
to taste

sea salt flakes and freshly ground
black pepper

heat from the oil with each fry), for 2–3 minutes until golden and crisp.
Remove and drain on kitchen paper.

Season with salt and serve hot with the bravas sauce.

NUTS

Nuts, nuts, my kingdom for some nuts! Well, not quite…but **they really are superb with a cocktail**. There are no portion sizes here. I've seen these devoured by very few and (strangely) ignored by many. So *I leave it to your judgement*.

ROSEMARY AND CHILLI-ROASTED WALNUTS

200g (7oz) walnut halves

½ tablespoon olive oil

½ tablespoon unsalted butter

2 teaspoons caster sugar

1 teaspoon cayenne pepper

1 small rosemary sprig, leaves only, finely chopped, plus extra to garnish

sea salt flakes

Preheat the oven to 180°C (350°F), Gas Mark 4. Spread the walnuts out on a baking sheet and toast in the oven for 5–8 minutes, or until crisp. Keep an eye on them, as they can burn quickly. Remove from the oven and set aside.

Heat the olive oil and butter in a frying pan over a medium heat and, when the butter has melted, add the sugar, cayenne pepper and rosemary. Stir until the ingredients are well combined and the sugar has melted. Add the walnuts and stir to coat thoroughly.

Remove from the heat. Transfer to a bowl, add a pinch of sea salt flakes and mix. Leave to cool. Serve with a sprinkle of salt and rosemary.

SALTED ALMONDS

If you don't do anything else at all, just make these. There is nothing like a salted almond with a Dry Martini. Heaven.

200g (7oz) blanched almonds

½ teaspoon unsalted butter, softened

fine sea salt flakes

Preheat the oven to 140°C (275°F), Gas Mark 1. Place the almonds on a baking sheet and, with your hands, generously coat them all over with the butter. Bake for 25–30 minutes, checking every now and then and giving them a shake, until they are honey blonde.

Remove from the oven and place immediately on to a sheet of greaseproof paper. Salt them generously straight away, then crumple up the paper a little and leave to cool.

Transfer to a bowl, sprinkle with the salt left on the paper and serve.

PAYON'S PEANUTS

You can put these together in minutes – so no excuses.

200g (7oz) salted peanuts

½ lime, cut into tiny slivers

2 spring onions, green parts only, finely chopped

1 large red chilli, deseeded and finely chopped

Mix all the ingredients together in a small bowl. Serve at once.

FRITTERS, PARCELS AND PUFFS

FESTIVE SAUSAGE ROLLS

What's a party without a sausage roll? Especially when it comes to feeding the family at Christmas. *Everyone loves these, warm from the oven and smelling of good times…* Here I've customized a traditional sausage roll recipe with a festive twist. You can also try out my recipe for a vegetarian version on the next page.

MAKES 24

400g (14oz) sausagemeat (use your favourite sausages, skinned, if you like)

60g (2¼oz) cooked and peeled chestnuts, roughly chopped

1 teaspoon dried sage

4 thyme sprigs, leaves only

a good grating of fresh nutmeg

1 tablespoon vegetable oil, plus 1 teaspoon and extra for greasing

1 onion, finely chopped

1 sheet of ready-rolled puff pastry

1 egg, lightly beaten with 1 tablespoon milk

sea salt flakes and freshly ground black pepper

Preheat the oven to 180°C (350°F), Gas Mark 4, and lightly grease a baking sheet. Mix together the sausagemeat, chestnuts, herbs and nutmeg in a large bowl.

In a hot frying pan, heat the 1 tablespoon oil and cook the onion until just soft. Allow to cool a little, then add to the sausage mixture and season with salt and pepper. Use your hands to combine all the ingredients really well.

Heat the remaining oil in a clean frying pan and fry off a tiny piece of the sausage mixture. Taste and adjust the seasoning, if necessary.

Unroll the sheet of puff pastry and place on the prepared baking sheet. Using a sharp knife, cut it in half lengthways. Divide the sausage mixture in half and lay a long "pipeline" in the centre along the length of each piece of pastry. Brush the pastry edges with the egg wash, then fold the dough over the sausage mixture, seal the edges and crimp with the tines of a fork. Brush all over with more egg wash and refrigerate for 10 minutes.

Bake for 25–30 minutes until cooked through, golden brown and crisp. Remove from the oven and leave to cool for a minute or so before cutting each roll into 12 pieces. Serve warm.

VEGETARIAN "SAUSAGE" ROLLS

The joy of sausage rolls shouldn't only be reserved for the meat eaters among us! **These savoury morsels go down very well with everyone**. You may end up with some extra mixture – it is delicious on toast for a light lunch or supper.

MAKES 24

2 tablespoons olive oil, plus extra for greasing

1 onion, finely chopped

1 celery stick, finely chopped

4 garlic cloves, finely chopped

50g (1¾oz) butter

500g (1lb 2oz) mixed mushrooms, chopped

10g (¼oz) dried porcini mushrooms, soaked and drained (soaking water reserved)

6 sage leaves, chopped

100g (3½oz) baby spinach

60g (2¼oz) cooked and peeled chestnuts, roughly chopped

50g (1¾oz) Stilton cheese, crumbled

1 sheet of ready-rolled puff pastry

1 egg, lightly beaten with 1 tablespoon milk

sea salt flakes and freshly ground black pepper

Preheat the oven to 180°C (350°F), Gas Mark 4, and lightly grease a baking sheet.

Heat the oil in a frying pan, add the onion and cook, stirring, until translucent. Add the celery and continue to cook until soft. Finally, add the garlic and cook for a couple more minutes until fragrant. Remove from the pan and set aside.

Now, cook the mushrooms. Melt half the butter in the pan, then add the mushrooms, including the porcini, in batches, and cook, stirring, until each batch releases its water and the water evaporates. You will need to add the rest of the butter as you add more mushrooms. When all their liquid has evaporated, add the sage and cook for maybe a minute or two, then add the spinach and allow that to wilt. Add a splash of the reserved mushroom soaking water if the mixture looks a little dry. Season with salt and pepper, then add the chestnuts and cheese. Leave to cool.

Unroll the sheet of puff pastry and place on the prepared baking sheet. Using a sharp knife, cut it in half lengthways. Divide the mushroom mixture in half and lay a long "pipeline" in the centre along the length of each piece of pastry. Brush the pastry edges with the egg wash, then fold the dough over the mushroom mixture, seal the edges and crimp with the tines of a fork. Brush all over with more egg wash and refrigerate for 10 minutes.

Bake for 25–30 minutes until golden brown and crisp. Remove from the oven and leave to cool for a minute or so before cutting each roll into 12. Serve warm.

Kay's Tip...

For the mixed mushrooms, you can use any kind – test out different combinations of your favourites.

SMALL TUNA-FILLED PASTRIES
FROM GALICIA

I'll admit it. This recipe is a bit of a cheat. I was craving these flavours and didn't have the patience to make the pastry from scratch. *Voilà*: my handy roll of chilled puff pastry came into play – and *it proved a light and easy way of recapturing some Galician sunshine.*

MAKES 24

2 tablespoons olive oil

1 onion, finely chopped

1 red pepper, cored, deseeded and finely chopped

2 garlic cloves, finely chopped

200g (7oz) tomatoes, skinned and finely chopped

150g (5½oz) can tuna in olive oil, drained

½ teaspoon mild paprika

1 good flat leaf parsley sprig, finely chopped

12 fat green olives, pitted and chopped

1 egg, hard-boiled, shelled and finely chopped (optional)

2 sheets of ready-rolled puff pastry

beaten egg, to glaze

sea salt flakes and freshly ground black pepper

Heat the olive oil in a frying pan, add the onion and red pepper and sauté until softened. Add the garlic and cook for a further few minutes, then add the tomatoes and cook until all is well combined and some of the excess liquid has evaporated. Flake in the tuna and season with the paprika, parsley, salt and pepper. Stir in the olives and the egg, if using. Taste and adjust the seasoning, if necessary. Leave to cool completely.

Preheat the oven to 200°C (400°F), Gas Mark 6, and line a baking sheet with nonstick baking paper.

Unroll the sheets of puff pastry and roll them out a little. Using a pastry cutter or a template, stamp out 8–10cm (3¼–4-inch) rounds. Fill each one with a spoonful of the mixture and fold into a half-moon shape, sealing the edges well. Decorate with the tines of a fork, if you like. Don't overfill, as they might burst!

Place the pastries on the lined baking sheet and brush all over with the beaten egg. Bake for 20–25 minutes until golden brown and puffed up. Serve hot or at room temperature.

QUICK CURRY PUFFS

This is not a traditional recipe for curry puffs – crispy pastry parcels full of mild curried chicken and potato – but **it works beautifully** and takes the hassle out of making fiddly pastry and deep-frying it. The results? *A lighter, brighter snack.*

MAKES 36–45

2 coriander roots, cut into chunks

2 garlic cloves, peeled

2 tablespoons vegetable oil

3 tablespoons light soy sauce

3 tablespoons water

2 tablespoons sugar

1 heaped tablespoon curry powder

1 onion, finely chopped

200g (7oz) boneless, skinless chicken thighs, finely chopped or coarsely minced

200g (7oz) potato, boiled and chopped

1 tablespoon chopped coriander

3 sheets of ready-rolled puff pastry

beaten egg, to glaze

sea salt flakes and freshly ground white pepper

Using a pestle and mortar, grind the coriander roots, garlic and a pinch of salt to a smooth paste. Heat the oil in a wok or frying pan until hot, add the paste and cook, stirring all the time, until it's very fragrant – only a few seconds. Add the soy sauce, measured water, sugar and curry powder and cook for another minute.

Add the onion, chicken and potato and simmer for a few minutes, stirring now and then, until the chicken is cooked through, adding a splash of water if it's looking a bit dry. Taste and add more salt if necessary – it should be sweet, a little spicy and salty and a little moist. Leave to cool, then add the chopped coriander and a good few grinds of white pepper.

Preheat the oven to 200°C (400°F), Gas Mark 6, and line a baking sheet with nonstick baking paper. Using a pastry cutter or a template, cut out 36–45 little rounds from the puff pastry sheets, about 7–8cm (2¾–3¼ inches) in diameter. Place a teaspoonful of the chicken mixture on each round, wet the edges of the pastry and fold over to make half-moon shapes, crimping the edges of the pastry as you go or using the tines of a fork to decoratively seal each one – they will taste delicious either way!

Place the parcels on the lined baking sheet and brush all over with the beaten egg. Bake for 20–25 minutes, or until golden brown and puffed up. Serve warm or at room temperature.

Kay's Tip...

You can also make these in advance and reheat them. Just preheat the oven to 180°C (350°F), Gas Mark 4, and bake for 8–10 minutes until crisp and hot through.

PRAWN FRITTERS
FROM JEREZ

When I tasted these at Bar Juanito in Jerez, they blew my mind – hot, flaky circles of light batter and shrimp, fried to crisp perfection. **Make extras, as they will all go**. In Cádiz, they make these with *camarones*, small whole shrimp that you can eat shell-on. I have had success with both brown shrimps (really good) and regular small prawns. The secret is to keep the oil at as constant a temperature as you can: *you need the inside cooked and the outside golden – not burned*!

MAKES 12–16

500g (1lb 2oz) raw peeled brown shrimps or small prawns

125g (4½oz) plain flour

125g (4½oz) gram or chickpea flour

300ml (½ pint) very cold water

2 tablespoons finely chopped flat leaf parsley

1 onion, very finely chopped

olive oil, for frying

sea salt flakes and freshly ground black pepper

lemon wedges, to serve

If using small prawns, chop them roughly and set aside.

In a cool bowl, mix the two types of flour. Add the measured water a little at a time until you have a batter with the consistency of single cream. Add the prawns or brown shrimps, parsley and onion. Season with a little salt and pepper and set aside.

Heat a wide heavy-based frying pan, add some olive oil – you will need a depth of about 2cm (¾ inch) – and heat it up.

Stir the batter again and drop 2 tablespoonfuls at a time into the pan, using a fish slice to gently press down and flatten each of them. When the edges start changing colour, flip them carefully. Cook very quickly, until the underside is just done. Remove from the pan with a slotted spoon or fish slice and pop on to some kitchen paper to drain. Like drop scones, sometimes the first one doesn't turn out quite as well as you'd hoped. Don't worry. All will be well thereafter. Serve hot, with lemon wedges.

CATALAN SALT COD FRITTERS

The recipe for these fluffy, chewy and **utterly delicious fritters** comes from Colman Andrews's *Catalan Cuisine*. He in turn got it *from Hispània, an acclaimed restaurant north of Barcelona.*

MAKES ABOUT 18

500g (1lb 2oz) salt cod, cut into pieces

1 bay leaf

2 medium potatoes, peeled and thinly sliced

2 garlic cloves, finely chopped

½ tablespoon finely chopped flat leaf parsley

vegetable oil, for deep-frying

sea salt flakes and freshly ground black pepper

For the batter

300ml (½ pint) water

2 tablespoons olive oil

60g (2¼oz) plain flour

3 eggs

To desalt the salt cod, place it in a bowl, cover with fresh water and leave to soak in the fridge for about 48 hours. Change the water 4 times during the soaking period.

Drain the cod, then put in a saucepan with the bay leaf and cover with fresh cold water. Place over a medium heat and heat until just below boiling point, then cover, remove from the heat and leave to stand for about 10 minutes. Remove the cod, reserving the water, and leave to cool. When cold, remove the skin and bones, then flake the fish with a fork.

Meanwhile, cook the potatoes in the reserved water until tender, then drain and set aside.

In a large bowl, mash the cod, potatoes, garlic and parsley together. Season with salt and pepper to taste.

To make the batter, bring the measured water and olive oil to the boil in a clean saucepan. Remove from the heat and slowly beat in the flour until you have a batter. Beat in the eggs, one at a time, then mix the cod mixture into the batter. Cook the mixture over a low heat until it thickens enough for a spoonful to hold its shape when you form it into a ball. Leave to cool, then form the mixture into squash-ball-sized fritters.

Heat the vegetable oil in a deep-fat fryer or deep saucepan to 190°C (375°F), or until a cube of bread turns golden in 30 seconds. Gently deep-fry the fritters, in batches, until they are a deep golden brown. Remove and drain on kitchen paper. Serve piping hot.

Kay's Tip...

More of a confession than a tip, but this recipe works perfectly well with canned crab! It also halves perfectly, so I'll sometimes whip up a half-batch with canned crab for a quick kitchen supper.

NOT QUITE MARYLAND CRAB CAKES

Crab cakes always get a reaction – I've been at events where people throng at the doors to the kitchens just to snaffle them fresh off the serving plates. But I can never decide between the classic Maryland version or something a little more Cajun. *This is a bit of a compromise between the two.*

MAKES ABOUT 36

1 egg

¼ teaspoon mustard powder

2 teaspoons Worcestershire sauce

2 tablespoons mayonnaise

finely grated zest of ½ lemon

1 teaspoon fresh lemon juice

½–1 teaspoon cayenne pepper

1 tablespoon Dijon mustard

25g (1oz) butter, melted

1 tablespoon chopped parsley

1 heaped teaspoon Old Bay Seasoning

50g (1¾oz) crushed Ritz crackers

500g (1lb 2oz) good-quality cooked crab meat

4 tablespoons vegetable oil

Chipotle Mayonnaise (see page 103), to serve

Line a baking sheet with nonstick baking paper. Place the egg in a mixing bowl with the mustard powder, Worcestershire sauce, mayonnaise, lemon zest and juice, cayenne, Dijon mustard, melted butter, parsley, Old Bay Seasoning and crushed crackers. Mix well to combine. Gently fold in the crab meat, being careful not to break up the lumps.

Shape the mixture into about 36 small patties and place on the lined baking sheet. Refrigerate for about 30 minutes to firm up the patties a little.

Heat the oil in a large nonstick frying pan until hot and fry the crab cakes for 5–6 minutes, a few at a time, turning them gently, until golden brown and cooked through. Drain on kitchen paper and serve with cocktail forks, with Chipotle Mayonnaise to dip your crab cakes into.

DEEP-FRIED CROQUETTES
FLAVOURED WITH SPICY 'NDUJA SAUSAGE

'Nduja is one of my favourite Italian ingredients. It is a **soft spicy sausage from Calabria**, the place where Italian food becomes seriously spicy. They love chillies there. And 'nduja is riddled with the little things. Note, however, that *some 'ndujas are spicier than others…*

MAKES 18–24

500g (1lb 2oz) floury potatoes (I favour King Edward), peeled and chopped

2 tablespoons olive oil

55g (2oz) 'nduja sausage, skinned if in casing

a good squeeze of lemon juice

2 eggs, beaten

100g (3½oz) fine dried breadcrumbs

vegetable oil, for deep-frying

sea salt flakes and freshly ground black pepper

Line a baking sheet with nonstick baking paper. Boil the potatoes in a large saucepan of lightly salted water until tender. Drain and mash with the olive oil. When fairly smooth, add the 'nduja sausagemeat and mash until you get a nice smooth, uniform texture. Add the lemon juice, salt and pepper and taste. Adjust the seasoning to taste.

Using your hands, roll the mixture into small log shapes, placing them on the lined baking sheet as you go. Cover gently and refrigerate until you are ready to cook.

Remove the "logs" from the fridge. Dip them into the beaten eggs and then into the breadcrumbs.

Meanwhile, in a deep-fat fryer or deep saucepan, heat the vegetable oil to 180°C (350°F), or until a cube of bread turns golden in 30 seconds. Gently deep-fry the croquettes, in batches, until crisp and golden. Remove and drain on kitchen paper. Serve, if possible, while they're still hot.

LETICIA'S BLUE CHEESE CROQUETTES

These creamy croquettes come from my friend Leticia Sánchez, from Badajoz in southern Spain. She tells me she created them as **a lighter alternative to traditional ham croquettes**. She has achieved her goal! *They are delicious, especially with a cold glass of Palo Cortado.*

MAKES 12–16

2 tablespoons olive oil

4 onions, halved and finely sliced

150g (5½oz) blue cheese (I like Roquefort), crumbled

3 heaped tablespoons cream cheese

4 tablespoons plain flour

400ml (14fl oz) milk (you might not need it all)

dried breadcrumbs, to coat

4 eggs, beaten

vegetable oil, for deep-frying

Heat the olive oil in a heavy-based saucepan, add the onions and cook over a low heat until soft and starting to turn golden. Add the blue cheese and stir through gently. After 3–4 minutes, add the cream cheese and let it cook for another 4–5 minutes. Add the flour and stir constantly until it comes together, almost like a dough.

Start adding the milk a little at a time, stirring as you do so, until you get a silky-smooth béchamel of sorts. Remove from the heat and leave to cool slightly, then cover and refrigerate for at least 2 hours or preferably overnight.

Remove the cheese mixture from the fridge and shape into balls or log shapes – Leticia likes to use 2 dessertspoons to form quenelle shapes. Roll the croquettes in the breadcrumbs, gently dip them into the beaten eggs, then give them another roll in the breadcrumbs.

In a deep-fat fryer or deep saucepan, heat the vegetable oil to 190°C (375°F), or until a cube of bread turns golden in 30 seconds. Gently deep-fry the croquettes, in batches, until deep golden brown. Remove and drain on kitchen paper. Serve immediately.

BAKES
AND SLICES

PISSALADIÈRE

Traditionally, this southern French tart is made with a dough that's very much like a pizza, but this **quick and easy version** is just as delicious. I always have ready-rolled puff pastry in the fridge or freezer – *it can be an absolute lifesaver when there is a last-minute get-together.*

MAKES 12–16 SQUARES

2 tablespoons olive oil

50g (1¾oz) butter

3 large red onions, finely sliced

a good pinch of sugar

2 garlic cloves, chopped

6 thyme sprigs

1 sheet of ready-rolled puff pastry

12 anchovy fillets, drained

12 pitted black olives

beaten egg, to glaze

sea salt flakes and freshly ground black pepper

Heat the oil and butter in a large saucepan. Add the onions and turn the heat down low. Let the onions cook slowly, stirring and turning every now and then, until they are deep golden and soft – 20–30 minutes. Add the sugar and stir through, then add the garlic and the leaves of 4 of the thyme sprigs and cook for a further few minutes. You want the onions to be meltingly tender. Season with a little salt and plenty of pepper and leave to cool.

Preheat the oven to 200°C (400°F), Gas Mark 6, and line a baking sheet with nonstick baking paper.

Unroll the puff pastry sheet and place on the lined baking sheet. Using a sharp knife, make a cut (but not all the way through) along the edges of the pastry, about 2cm (¾ inch) in from the edge. This will give the pie a nice crusty raised edge. Prick the inside of the oblong with a fork.

Gently pile the cooked onion mixture on to the pastry, keeping within the cut lines.

Criss-cross the anchovies in a diamond pattern all over the onions. Place an olive in the middle of each diamond. Scatter with the remaining thyme sprigs. Season lightly.

Brush the pastry edges with the beaten egg, then bake for 20–30 minutes until the pastry is risen and golden brown. Serve warm, cut into squares.

CRAB, SAFFRON AND GRUYÈRE TART

This is, essentially, a quiche that has grown up and moved abroad…**sophisticated, creamy and fragrant with saffron**. It's best served at just above room temperature – definitely not cold – so it still has *a little wobble and warmth*.

SERVES 12

2 eggs plus 1 egg yolk, lightly beaten

200ml (7fl oz) double cream

a pinch of freshly grated nutmeg

a large pinch of saffron threads

170g (6oz) can crab meat, drained

100g (3½oz) Gruyère cheese, grated

sea salt flakes and freshly ground black pepper

rocket, to garnish (optional)

For the pastry

225g (8oz) plain flour

110g (3¾oz) cold unsalted butter, cut into cubes, plus extra for greasing

a small glass of iced water

Preheat the oven to 190°C (375°F), Gas Mark 5, and grease a 36 x 12cm (14 x 4½-inch) rectangular or 20cm (8-inch) round loose-bottomed flan tin.

To make the pastry, sift the flour into a bowl and rub in the butter with your fingertips until the mixture resembles fine breadcrumbs. Add a good pinch of salt and stir it in, then add the iced water, a teaspoonful at a time, until the mixture just comes together into a dough. If you add too much water you'll get a hard pastry.

Push the dough straight into the greased flan tin, easing it around gently with your knuckles until it is evenly covering the base and sides. Line the pastry case with nonstick baking paper and weight it down with baking beans. Bake blind for about 10 minutes, then remove the beans and paper and return the tart case to the oven for a further 5 minutes. Leave to cool.

To make the filling, mix the eggs and the yolk, the cream, nutmeg and saffron together in a large bowl and season with salt and pepper. Beat the mixture with a hand-held electric whisk until thoroughly combined, then leave to stand for 20 minutes. Beat again, then carefully stir in the crab and grated cheese.

Pour the filling into the flan tin and bake for 30–40 minutes until the pastry is golden brown and the filling is domed, burnished and puffy. Leave to cool to room temperature, or just above, before garnishing with rocket, if you like, cutting into slices and serving.

FOCACCIA
WITH OLIVES AND ROSEMARY

I had the great pleasure of meeting *The Great British Bake Off* **finalist Richard Burr** over an excellent cooked breakfast at the Pen-y-Dre B&B before the Abergavenny Food Festival. He was there to demo his doughs; I was there with enough sherry to inebriate at least half of Wales; and naturally we got to asking each other what we were doing next. Which, for me, was my book *Aperitivo*. "Got a focaccia recipe?" says I. "Sure," says he. And here it is. This recipe appears in his brilliant book **BIY: Bake It Yourself**.

MAKES 2 LOAVES

500g (1lb 2oz) strong white bread flour

2 teaspoons salt

1 tablespoon fast-action dried yeast

50ml (2fl oz) olive oil, plus extra for greasing, kneading, shaping and drizzling

350ml (12fl oz) water

20 pitted green olives, halved

a few rosemary sprigs, leaves only

sea salt flakes and freshly ground black pepper

Line 2 baking sheets with nonstick baking paper and oil a plastic container that holds at least 2 litres (3½ pints).

Put the flour into a bowl and add the salt and the yeast on opposite sides from each other, then stir together with a wooden spoon. Add the oil and measured water, then bring together to form a wet dough.

Pour 2 tablespoons of olive oil on to your work surface and knead the dough on it for a good 10 minutes. You might need to add a little more flour, but this is supposed to be a wet dough – prepare to get a little oily.

Place the dough in the oiled plastic container, cover with clingfilm and leave to prove in a warm place until doubled in size. Now turn out the dough on to an oiled work surface and cut it in half. Richard's tip is to oil the blades of 2 long knives. Use one to cut the dough, then slide the other in alongside it to push the 2 halves apart. Gently place each half on its own lined baking sheet. Form each one into a lozenge shape, cover with plastic bags and leave to prove in a warm place for another 45 minutes. Don't let the plastic touch the dough.

Preheat the oven to 220°C (425°F), Gas Mark 7. Meanwhile, uncover the dough, then press the olive halves firmly into the dough,

scatter with the rosemary leaves, drizzle with olive oil and season with salt and pepper.

Bake for 20–25 minutes until golden, then transfer to wire racks to cool. Finally, drizzle with more olive oil before cutting and...devouring.

MINI CORNBREADS
WITH BACON, CHILLI AND CHEESE

Here's a little **Southern kick** for your cocktail party. These little morsels are seriously moreish, so *you may need to make double*...

MAKES 24

4 streaky bacon rashers

125g (4½oz) cornmeal

110g (3¾oz) plain flour

1 tablespoon caster sugar

1 teaspoon salt

1 heaped tablespoon baking powder

65ml (2¼fl oz) vegetable oil or melted butter, plus extra for greasing

100ml (3½fl oz) milk

100ml (3½fl oz) buttermilk

1 large egg, lightly beaten

1 jalapeño chilli, deseeded and finely chopped

25g (1oz) Cheddar cheese, grated

unsalted butter, softened, beaten with chopped mixed herbs and sea salt flakes, to serve

Preheat the oven to 200°C (400°F), Gas Mark 6, and lightly grease 2 x 12-hole mini muffin tins or 1 x 24-hole mini muffin tin. When the oven is hot, put the streaky bacon on a baking sheet and bake for about 12 minutes, or until crispy. Remove and leave to cool on kitchen paper, then crumble it into small pieces and set aside.

Combine all the dry ingredients in a large bowl. Add the wet ingredients, mixing together thoroughly until you have a soft, dropping consistency – you may need to add a little more milk or buttermilk to achieve this. Stir in the chilli, bacon and cheese and mix well.

Pour the mixture into the prepared tin and bake for 20–25 minutes until golden brown and risen.

Leave to cool in the tin for a few minutes before serving warm with some beaten seasoned butter.

SMOKED MACKEREL PÂTÉ

Sometimes when it's busy, especially at and around Christmas, you want – scratch that – you **need** easy recipes that deliver **proper deliciousness**. *This fits the bill.*

MAKES 650G (1LB 7OZ)

460g (1lb) smoked mackerel fillets, skinned and flaked

200ml (7fl oz) crème fraîche

2 teaspoons grated horseradish (The English Provender Co. make a good one)

1 tablespoon fresh lemon juice

1 teaspoon English mustard

1 tablespoon chopped chives, plus extra to garnish

sea salt flakes and freshly ground black pepper

To serve

warm fingers of toast or blinis

lemon wedges (optional)

Pop everything except the chopped chives into a blender or food processor and blend until smooth. Stir in the chives and season with pepper. Taste, then season with salt, if necessary – smoked mackerel can be quite salty enough already sometimes. Cover and refrigerate until slightly chilled.

Serve slightly chilled on warm fingers of toast or blinis, then top with a grinding of black pepper and some chopped chives. Serve with lemon wedges for squeezing over.

EACH RECIPE MAKES 12

BRUSCHETTE

The sheer simplicity of bruschette – basically, **toast with lovely toppings** – belies their utter deliciousness. But it all comes down to the quality of the bread and its mate…so here I've suggested two toppings. Ideally, the bread should be toasted on a hot griddle, although *I'll use the toaster if I'm in a hurry.*

ROQUEFORT AND MARMALADE ONION BRUSCHETTA

Yes, marmalade onions, not the usual onion marmalade. It's quick, easy and absolutely delicious.

15g (½oz) unsalted butter

1 tablespoon olive oil

2 onions, halved and sliced

2 tablespoons good-quality marmalade

a good pinch of marjoram leaves (optional)

6 slices of sourdough bread

150–200g (5½–7oz) Roquefort cheese

sea salt flakes and freshly ground black pepper

Heat the butter and oil in a saucepan over a low heat until melted and hot. Add the onions and cook slowly for about 20 minutes until they are soft and melting but still retain texture. You may want to turn up the heat at the end for some colour, but make sure they don't burn.

Add a pinch of salt and a good grinding of pepper, then take the onions off the heat and immediately stir in the marmalade until well combined. Add the marjoram leaves, if using, and stir again. Taste and adjust the seasoning, if necessary. Leave to cool, then cover and refrigerate until ready to serve.

Toast the bread slices. Smear each piece with a liberal amount of Roquefort, then top with some marmalade onions and serve.

RICOTTA, POMEGRANATE AND THYME BRUSCHETTA

Bright ruby jewels on a snowy ricotta backdrop…

6 slices of sourdough bread

1 garlic clove, halved

200–250g (7–9oz) ricotta cheese

100g (3½oz) pomegranate seeds

a small handful of thyme leaves

sea salt flakes and freshly ground black pepper

Toast the bread and rub it with the garlic while it's still warm. Smear the slices with the ricotta. Sprinkle with the pomegranate seeds and thyme leaves, season with salt and pepper and serve.

Kay's Tip…

Choose very good-quality sourdough bread to make bruschetta. You could use baguettes instead, in which case, each recipe is enough to top 18 slices.

VODKA AND CARAWAY CURED
SALMON ON RYE

A Lithuanian take on the traditional Scandinavian gravadlax, **try it with chilled shots of good vodka.** The vodka and caraway make for a delicious combination, and the beetroot pickle lends a fresh tartness. *Don't forget to start two days before you want to eat it.*

MAKES 35 CANAPÉS, OR 12–16 LARGER PORTIONS

1kg (2lb 4oz) very fresh, centre-cut salmon fillet

2 teaspoons black peppercorns, crushed

½ heaped tablespoon caraway seeds, lightly crushed

75g (2½oz) Maldon sea salt flakes

75g (2½oz) caster sugar

75ml (2½fl oz) vodka

20g (¾oz) dill, chopped, plus extra to garnish

To serve

Quick Beetroot Pickle (see opposite) or lemon wedges

rye bread

Cut the salmon in half across the fillet, remove any pin bones and set aside on a board, skin-side down.

Place the crushed peppercorns in a bowl with the caraway seeds, salt and sugar, then mix in the vodka. Evenly spread the mixture on to the flesh side of the salmon, pressing it in until you have used it all up. Lay the dill evenly over the surface of the fish. Now sandwich the 2 pieces of salmon together, skin-side out, so that the curing sides are touching each other. Tie with kitchen string, tucking in any filling that spills out, then wrap the fish tightly in clingfilm – I like to wrap it twice so that it is really secure.

Place the parcel in a dish to catch any escaping liquids and refrigerate for 48 hours. You can weight the salmon down with something heavy if you like. And, if you remember, you can turn it a couple of times, but it doesn't really make that much difference.

Remove the salmon from the clingfilm and gently wipe off the excess dill and cure. Place the fish, skin-side down, on a board and scatter with a little extra dill.

Serve the salmon with the beetroot pickle on the side and slices of good rye bread. Or assemble the canapés yourself by thinly slicing the salmon, placing it on rye bread and topping it with a little of the pickle. You could also serve it with lemon wedges instead.

QUICK
BEETROOT
PICKLE

4 small raw beetroot, grated

4 tablespoons red wine vinegar

4 tablespoons olive oil

**sea salt flakes and freshly
ground black pepper**

Place all the ingredients in
a large bowl, cover and leave
for about 2 hours in the fridge,
then drain off the liquid
thoroughly before serving the
grated beetroot with the salmon.
This can be made a few hours
before you want to serve it.

AVOCADO TOASTS
WITH ANCHOVIES

Mexico meets Spain as the creamy avocado sets off the salty anchovy. *My favourite!*

MAKES 8

2 avocados, halved, stoned, peeled and diced

2 garlic cloves, finely chopped

2 small tomatoes, deseeded and diced

1 hot red chilli, deseeded and chopped

½ small red onion, finely chopped

juice of ½ lemon

2 tablespoons chopped coriander, plus 1 teaspoon

8 slices of large baguette, lightly toasted

8 good Spanish anchovy fillets, drained

extra virgin olive oil, for drizzling

sea salt flakes and freshly ground black pepper

Mash the avocados in a bowl, then add the garlic, tomatoes, chilli, onion, lemon juice and the 2 tablespoons coriander. Season with a little salt and pepper.

Divide the avocado between the slices of toasted bread. Top each with an anchovy, drizzle with extra virgin olive oil and sprinkle over the remaining teaspoon of coriander.

CHICKEN LIVER PÂTÉ
WITH APPLES, SAGE AND CALVADOS

Creamy and rich with a tang of apple, this is a winner at any event. *Serve with slices of fresh French bread or crisp toast points.*

SERVES 24

750g (1lb 10oz) chicken livers

200g (7oz) butter

2 tablespoons olive oil

4 apples (preferably Cox's), peeled, cored and cut into chunks

8 sage leaves, roughly torn, plus 2 more to garnish

4 tablespoons Calvados or brandy

250ml (9fl oz) double cream

sea salt flakes and freshly ground black pepper

To serve

slices of fresh baguette or toast

cornichons

pickled onions

Pick over the chicken livers and remove any fat, gristle or green bits, then chop them into bite-sized pieces and set aside.

Heat 50g (1¾oz) of the butter and half the oil in a nonstick frying pan over a medium heat until the butter foams, then add the apples. Sauté them for 5–10 minutes until golden and soft. You want the wooden spoon to cut through them with ease. Transfer to a plate and set aside.

Season the livers. Heat another 50g (1¾oz) of the butter and the remaining oil in the pan and, when it's hot, add the livers. (You may have to do this in batches, depending on the size of your pan.) Cook the livers through (no pink bits in this recipe) – it could take anywhere from 10–15 minutes. Just keep prodding them until the juices run clear.

Return the apples to the pan, add the sage and combine well, letting it all bubble. Add another 25g (1oz) of the butter and stir it through until it is melted and bubbling. Now carefully add half the Calvados or brandy and flambé by lighting the alcohol fumes with a match. Take it off the heat and let the flames die.

Set aside to cool for 5–10 minutes, then transfer the mixture to a blender or food processor and blend, adding the cream slowly while the machine is running. Stop now and then to scrape down the sides and check the consistency – we want creamy with a little texture. Add the remaining Calvados or brandy and pulse briefly or stir in. Season with salt and pepper to taste.

Pour the pâté into a bowl or Mason jar and leave to cool, then cover the surface with a round of greaseproof paper. Place in the fridge to chill. When it's cold, melt the remaining butter in a small pan and set aside to allow the white solids to fall to the bottom. Arrange the 2 sage leaves artfully in the middle of the pâté, then pour over the clear clarified butter, leaving the white solids in the bottom of the pan. Cover and refrigerate until ready to serve. The pâté will keep for up to 4–5 days in the fridge. Serve with slices of baguette or toast, cornichons and pickled onions.

Kay's Tip...

This also works beautifully with the same amounts of duck livers, pears and Poire William liqueur.

COJONUDA Y COJONUDO
MORCILLA AND CHORIZO WITH FRIED QUAILS' EGGS

Hailing from Castile, these are, quite literally, the "*cojones*" of tapas! The words mean just what you think they do…But it can also mean brilliant or excellent – much as in English, if you add "the dog's". I suggest doing half and half. Yin and Yang.

MAKES 8

8 slices of large baguette, toasted

1 garlic clove, halved

2–3 tablespoons olive oil

4–8 slices of morcilla

8 quails' eggs

8 strips of bottled piquillo pepper

4–8 slices of chorizo

sea salt flakes and freshly ground black pepper

Rub each slice of toasted baguette with the halved garlic. Set aside.

For the Cojonuda

Heat half the olive oil in a heavy-based frying pan, add the morcilla and cook until just done on each side. Place on kitchen paper to drain. Meanwhile, in the same pan, fry 4 of the quails' eggs. Once they are done, place the morcilla on 4 slices of toast, top with the eggs and a strip of piquillo pepper, and season with salt and pepper.

For the Cojonudo

Follow the method above, replacing the morcilla with chorizo, but cooking the quails' eggs first to avoid discoloration.

PADRÓN PEPPER AND HAM
ON TOASTED BAGUETTE

A little crisp fried vegetable and some salty ham make this **a simple but effective snack**. Unique to the Padrón region of Galicia, the peppers are green, glossy torpedoes that are also a perfect accompaniment to a glass of something flinty – like a Manzanilla. Beware, though: while the majority of these peppers are fairly mild, every now and then one will come and bite you on the bottom! (As they say about Padrón peppers, "**unos pican y otros no**" – some are hot, others not.)

MAKES 8

2 tablespoons vegetable oil

8 Padrón peppers

8 slices of baguette, lightly toasted

1 garlic clove, halved

2 tomatoes, halved

8 slices of Serrano ham

coarse sea salt flakes

a drizzle of extra virgin olive oil (optional)

sea salt flakes and freshly ground black pepper

To make the fried Padrón peppers, heat the vegetable oil in a heavy-based frying pan until very hot, then carefully add the peppers. Fry them, turning occasionally, so that they start to "blister" and char a little. This will take about 3–5 minutes.

Meanwhile, rub the slices of toasted bread with the halved garlic clove, then rub with the halved tomatoes. Place the Serrano ham on the bread.

Remove the Padrón peppers from the pan with a slotted spoon on to a platter. Sprinkle with plenty of coarse sea salt flakes. Place on top of the Serrano ham and serve piping hot, drizzled with some good olive oil, if you like. Season with salt and pepper.

Kay's Tip...

Many recipes call for frying the peppers in olive oil. Please do so if you wish; I prefer vegetable oil because I can get it to a nice high temperature to really blister the peppers properly.

EACH RECIPE MAKES 8

BOCADILLOS – SMALL SANDWICHES

Now to clear things up: a **bocadillo** is a substantial Spanish Scooby snack – kind of a more delicate version of an American subway sandwich. The bread is thick and local – ciabatta makes a good substitute – and is sliced lengthways. For these canapé versions, I have made them smaller. But you could go full size and just cut them in half, for extra-hungry guests. *Sand-weeches*, or sandwiches, are made using modern sliced or unsliced bread. So there.

AUBERGINE CAVIAR WITH ANCHOVIES AND PRESERVED LEMONS

With a combination of textures and flavours, creamy aubergine, sharp lemons and salty anchovies make a satisfying snack.

2 aubergines

2 tablespoons extra virgin olive oil

1 tablespoon fresh lemon juice

1 tablespoon sherry vinegar

2 tablespoons chopped flat leaf parsley

1–2 teaspoons preserved lemon peel, finely chopped

a pinch of dried chilli flakes (optional)

16 anchovy fillets, drained

16 slices of square-cut ciabatta or rolls

sea salt flakes and freshly ground black pepper

Preheat the oven to 220°C (425°F), Gas Mark 7. Place the aubergines in the oven on a baking sheet and cook for about 1 hour, or until fork-soft. Remove from the oven and leave to cool slightly. When cool enough to handle, cut the aubergines in half and scoop out all the flesh into a bowl. Mash the flesh gently with all the other ingredients except for the anchovies and bread. Leave to cool to room temperature. Taste and adjust the seasoning.

Serve sandwiched between your chosen bread, with the anchovies criss-crossed on top.

GRILLED CHEESE WITH HAM AND HOT PEPPERS

This is a little bit of Americana, but with big Spanish flavours…more of a **sand-weech** than a **bocadillo** proper, but very tasty nonetheless.

2 tablespoons Dijon mustard

4 slices of good sourdough or country-style bread, crusts removed, halved if large

4 slices of Serrano ham

4 slices of Manchego cheese

4 guindilla chillies (see Kay's Tip)

2–4 tablespoons olive oil

Spread the Dijon mustard on 2 slices of the bread. Layer the ham, cheese and chillies evenly on top. Sandwich together with the remaining bread and press down tight.

Heat the olive oil in a heavy-based frying pan. Place the sandwiches, one at a time, in the hot oil and press them down lightly with a fish slice. Cook, flipping once, until brown and toasted and the cheese is oozing.

Remove from the pan, cut into 4cm (1½-inch) sand-weeches, if necessary, and serve.

Kay's Tip…
Guindillas are traditional Basque pickled chillies. Buy them in jars and enjoy.

TRAMEZZINI

Tramezzini are, for want of a better way of putting it, the same sort of sandwiches you might have with afternoon tea in England, except they are served with drinks. They are made with soft white sliced bread, which sometimes underwhelms those who have come to revere all things Italian food as artisan (don't worry...it WORKS). And they are wildly popular across northern Italy, especially in the Veneto. You will find them everywhere, from vending machines to the chicest speakeasy.

The word *tramezzino* translates as "a little something in between". It was coined by the poet Gabriele D'Annunzio to replace the word *sandwich* because...well...Mussolini banned it. Along with all the other non-Italian words in the language. Charming.

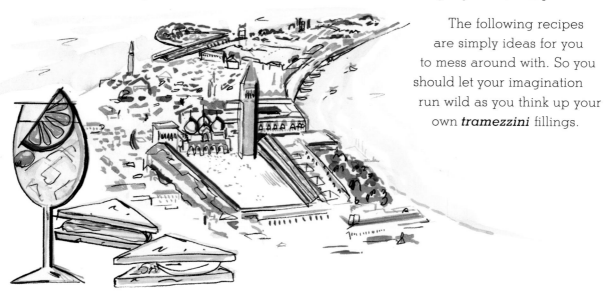

The following recipes are simply ideas for you to mess around with. So you should let your imagination run wild as you think up your own *tramezzini* fillings.

EACH RECIPE MAKES 4 TRIANGLES OR TRAMEZZINI

TUNA, EGG AND OLIVES

120g (4¼oz) tuna in oil, drained

2 tablespoons mayonnaise

a squeeze of lemon juice

4 slices of packaged white bread, crusts removed

4–6 pitted black olives, halved

1 egg, hard-boiled, shelled and sliced

sea salt flakes and freshly ground black pepper

In a small bowl, mix together the tuna and mayonnaise. Season with the lemon juice, salt and pepper. Layer on to 2 slices of the bread. Dot the olive halves on top, then add the egg slices. Season again, if you like. Top with the remaining 2 slices of bread. Cut in half diagonally to form 4 triangles.

CHICKEN AND CAPERS WITH AIOLI

1 boneless, skinless chicken breast, grilled or poached

2 tablespoons Aioli (see page 73)

1 tablespoon capers, rinsed, drained and chopped

½ tablespoon chopped flat leaf parsley

4 slices of packaged white bread, crusts removed

sea salt flakes and freshly ground black pepper

Shred the chicken breast. Pop the chicken into a bowl and add the aioli, capers and parsley. Season with salt and pepper. Layer on to 2 slices of the bread. Top with the remaining 2 slices. Cut in half diagonally to form 4 triangles.

HAM AND SAUTÉED MUSHROOMS

1 tablespoon olive oil

100g (3½oz) mushrooms, sliced

1 garlic clove, bashed in its skin

1 tablespoon chopped flat leaf parsley

4 slices of packaged white bread, crusts removed

1 tablespoon mayonnaise

4 slices of good-quality ham

sea salt flakes and freshly ground black pepper

Heat the oil in a heavy-based frying pan, add the mushrooms and sauté until they have let go of their liquid. Add the garlic and stir in well. Season with salt and pepper. Remove from the heat and leave to cool. When cool, remove the garlic clove and stir in the parsley. Taste and adjust the seasoning, if necessary.

Spread 2 slices of the bread with the mayonnaise. Layer on the ham and mushrooms. Place the remaining 2 slices of bread on top. Cut in half diagonally to form 4 triangles.

ROAST BEEF WITH HORSERADISH AND WATERCRESS

1 tablespoon mayonnaise

1 tablespoon crème fraîche

¼ teaspoon English mustard

1 teaspoon grated horseradish

a squeeze of lemon juice

4 slices of packaged white bread, crusts removed

2–4 slices of rare roast beef

a small handful of watercress

sea salt flakes and freshly ground black pepper

Mix together the mayonnaise, crème fraiche, mustard, horseradish and lemon juice. Season with salt and pepper. Spread this on to 2 slices of the bread. Top with the slices of beef and add a few sprigs of watercress. Place the remaining 2 slices of bread on top. Cut in half diagonally to form 4 triangles.

SMALL BITE-SIZED "CHEAT'S" PIZZAS
WITH 3 TOPPINGS

Okay. I admit it. I love these little bites so much that **I use a ready-made pizza dough**. Yes, I know, I know. But let's be honest here. We've all done it. I just can't wait for all that proving and rising, especially when preparing for a party. And sometimes a girl's in a hurry and needs some pizza. So shoot me. **You can top the pizzette with whatever you like**, but here are a few suggestions.

MAKES 16–18

plain flour, for dusting

2 x 220g (7¾oz) portions ready-made pizza dough (I like Northern Dough Co.), defrosted if frozen

Preheat the oven to 240°C (475°F), Gas Mark 9.

On a lightly floured surface, roll the 2 sets of dough out, one at a time, to about 5mm (¼ inch) thick. Using a 6cm (2½-inch) round cutter or template, punch out your little *pizzette*. Place them on a floured baking sheet.

Top with your choice of the following 3 toppings: *Bianche* (tomato-free "white" pizza, see right), classic *Margherita* (see opposite) or *Diavola e Acciughe* (which literally means "Devil and anchovy", see opposite) if you like it hot.

BIANCHE

For the topping

olive oil, for drizzling

250g (9oz) buffalo mozzarella cheese

4 rosemary sprigs, leaves only, chopped

50g (1¾oz) Parmesan cheese, freshly grated

sea salt flakes and freshly ground black pepper

Drizzle a little olive oil over each disc of dough.

Rip up the mozzarella and dot evenly over the *pizzette*. Add the rosemary and the Parmesan. Season with salt and pepper.

Add another drizzle of olive oil and bake (see left) for 10–15 minutes until they are golden brown and bubbling.

MARGHERITA

For the topping

olive oil, for drizzling

400g (14oz) can good-quality chopped tomatoes

1 teaspoon dried oregano

125g (4½oz) buffalo mozzarella cheese

sea salt flakes and freshly ground black pepper

basil leaves, to garnish

Drizzle each disc of dough with some olive oil.

Roughly crush up the chopped tomatoes, either with your hands or by pulsing in a food processor, retaining some texture. Add the oregano and season with salt and pepper.

Smear the tomato mixture over the *pizzette*. Tear up the mozzarella and dot over evenly. Add another drizzle of olive oil and bake (see opposite) for 10–15 minutes.

Garnish with some basil.

DIAVOLA E ACCIUGHE

For the topping

olive oil, for drizzling

400g (14oz) can good-quality chopped tomatoes

1 garlic clove, crushed

a good pinch of crushed dried chilli flakes (more if you like it hot)

125g (4½oz) buffalo mozzarella cheese

16–18 anchovy fillets, drained

16–18 pitted black olives, halved (optional)

½ teaspoon dried oregano

sea salt flakes and freshly ground black pepper

Drizzle a little olive oil over each disc of dough.

Roughly crush up the chopped tomatoes, either with your hands or by pulsing in a food processor, retaining some texture. Add the garlic and chilli flakes and season with salt and pepper.

Smear the tomato mixture over the *pizzette*. Tear up the mozzarella and scatter over evenly. Drape over the anchovies and dot with the olives, if using. Scatter over the dried oregano. Drizzle with a little more olive oil and bake (see opposite) for 10–15 minutes.

SERRANO HAM, ROQUEFORT, WALNUT AND GRAPE TOASTS

These are delicious served with a soup shot (see pages 94–97).

MAKES 8

8 slices of large baguette, toasted

1 garlic clove, halved

8 "smears" of Roquefort cheese

4 slices of Serrano ham, torn

8 green seedless grapes, halved

8–12 walnut halves, broken

Rub the slices of toasted bread with the garlic clove. Smear on a goodly amount of Roquefort cheese, then top with the torn Serrano ham, grape halves and walnut pieces.

POTATO, MANCHEGO AND SAFFRON TORTILLA

Golden morsels of eggy delight, wafting the scent of saffron and warm Spanish evenings through your home.

SERVES 8

4 eggs

a pinch of saffron threads

50g (1¾oz) Manchego cheese, grated, plus extra to serve (optional)

75g (2½oz) new potatoes

2 tablespoons olive oil

sea salt flakes and freshly ground black pepper

Break the eggs into a bowl, add the saffron and beat lightly. Add salt and pepper to taste and the Manchego, stir through and set aside.

Place the potatoes in a saucepan of lightly salted water and bring to the boil. Simmer for 8–10 minutes until *just* cooked, then remove from the heat, drain and refresh in cold water. Drain again and set aside to dry thoroughly, then cut into 5mm (¼-inch) thick slices.

Heat the oil in a small but sturdy tortilla pan or frying pan, about 16cm (6¼ inches) across, with a heatproof handle. Add the potatoes and cook for a few minutes, turning now and then, until golden and soft. You may have to do this in batches.

Pour the eggs over the potatoes and cook gently until set, using a spatula to pull back the edges to check that it's browning nicely.

When the bottom and sides are golden, and only the top has yet to set, place the pan under a preheated hot grill and cook until golden and puffy. Allow to cool slightly, then turn out on to a plate and scatter over some shavings of Manchego, if you like. Cut into wedges and serve warm or cold.

See a picture of this dish

PAGE 44

HERB AND CHEESE FRITTATA

An Italian frittata has more in common with a Spanish tortilla than it does a French omelette. They are cooked on both sides, slowly, until firm. Allegedly, some people flip them like pancakes. I think this is a recipe for disaster, and ends with egg all over the floor and a very happy dog; the best solution is to finish the top gently under the grill (how I miss an old-fashioned, eye-level grill), or to turn them with the aid of a separate lid or plate in the modern Spanish style.

SERVES 4–6

4 eggs

3 tablespoons grated Parmesan cheese

1 tablespoon torn basil leaves

1 tablespoon chopped flat leaf parsley

1 tablespoon chopped oregano leaves

25g (1oz) butter

sea salt flakes and freshly ground black pepper

Beat the eggs in a bowl until well combined, then add the cheese, herbs, salt and pepper, and beat again.

Melt the butter in a small but sturdy tortilla pan or frying pan, about 16cm (6¼ inches) across, with a heatproof handle if finishing under the grill. When it's foaming, add the egg mixture, turning down the heat to its lowest setting. Cook very gently until only the top of the frittata is still runny and then turn carefully with the aid of a lid and slide back into the pan to cook for another 45 seconds or so. Alternatively, finish under a preheated hot grill until just set.

Turn out on to a warm plate, cut into wedges and serve.

BIBLIOGRAPHY

Robert Vermeire, *Cocktails: How To Mix Them* (1922, available from Martino Fine Books, 2015)

Charles Schumann, *American Bar: The Artistry of Mixing Drinks* (Abbeville Press, 1995)

Harry Craddock, *The Savoy Cocktail Book* (1930, available from Girard & Stewart, 2015)

Talia Baiocchi and Leslie Pariseau, *Spritz* (Ten Speed Press, 2016)

Harry MacElhone, *Harry's ABC of Mixing Cocktails* (1922, available from Martino Fine Books, 2017)

Stanley Tucci and Felicity Blunt, with Kay Plunkett-Hogge, *The Tucci Table* (Orion, 2015)

Sam Hart, Eddie Hart and Nieves Barragán Mohacho, *Barrafina: A Spanish Cookbook* (Fig Tree, 2011)

Colman Andrews, *Catalan Cuisine* (Grub Street, 1997)

Richard Burr, *BIY: Bake It Yourself* (Quadrille, 2015)

GLOSSARY OF UK AND US TERMS

UK	US
aubergine	eggplant
bacon rashers	bacon slices
baking beans	pie weights
baking paper	parchment paper
beetroot	beet
biscuit	cookie
caster sugar	superfine sugar
chickpeas	garbanzo beans
chips (potato)	fries
clingfilm	plastic wrap
cocktail stick	toothpick
coriander	cilantro
courgette	zucchini
crisps (potato)	potato chips
double cream	heavy cream
dried chilli flakes	dried hot pepper flakes
fast-action dried yeast	active dry yeast
fine sieve	fine-mesh strainer
fish slice	spatula
flan tin	tart pan
floury potatoes	Russet potatoes
full-fat milk	whole milk
greaseproof paper	wax paper
griddle pan	grill pan
grill	broiler

UK	US
hand-held blender	immersion blender
hand-held electric whisk	hand-held electric beater
hob	stove-top
jug	pitcher
kitchen paper	paper towels
minced (meat)	ground (meat)
pastry	pastry dough
pastry case	pie shell
pastry cutter	cookie cutter
plain flour	all-purpose flour
polenta	cornmeal
pork belly	pork side
prawns	shrimp
red/orange pepper	red/orange bell pepper
rocket	arugula
sausagemeat	fresh pork sausage
single cream	pouring/light cream
sirloin steak	tenderloin steak
soda water	club soda
spatula	fish slice
spring onions	scallions
tea towel	dish towel
tin (cake/baking)	pan
tomato purée	tomato paste
wire rack	cooling rack

INDEX

An Hachette UK Company
www.hachette.co.uk

First published in Great Britain
in 2018 by Mitchell Beazley
a division of Octopus Publishing Group Ltd
Carmelite House, 50 Victoria Embankment
London EC4Y 0DZ
www.octopusbooks.co.uk

Some of the recipes in this book previously appeared
in *Make Mine a Martini*, *A Sherry and a Little Plate of
Tapas* and *Aperitivo*.

Text copyright © Kay Plunkett-Hogge 2018
Design, illustrations & photography © Octopus Publishing
Group Ltd 2018

Distributed in the US by Hachette Book Group
1290 Avenue of the Americas, 4th and 5th Floors
New York, NY 10104

Distributed in Canada by Canadian Manda Group
664 Annette St., Toronto, Ontario, Canada M6S 2C8

ISBN 978 1 78472 463 4

A CIP catalogue record for this book is available from the
British Library.

Printed and bound in China

10 9 8 7 6 5 4 3 2 1

Acknowledgments

Thanks to all the Octopi for your continued
support of drinks books. In particular Alison
Starling for coming up with this idea, Juliette
Norsworthy for her beautiful designing, Emily
Brickell for top editing and keeping things on
track and Allison Gonsalves for all manner of
brilliant production services.

Caroline Brown and the media team – *j'adore*.

Tamin Jones for excellent photography, and
Stephanie Howard for her invaluable assisting.
And the fragrant Kate Whitaker and her faithful
assistant Badger.

Abi Read for illustrating once again, and
somehow picturing what's going on in my
head but making it look even cooler.

Fred Hogge for excellent assisting, eating,
cooking and husbanding.

Maya and Ruffy for being kitchen dogs
extraordinaire.

And for kind contributors – many, many
thanks for your generosity: Colman Andrews,
Leticia Sanchez, Nick Cuthbert, Khun Jao
Fah, Felicity Blunt and Stanley Tucci, and
Richard Burr.

Publisher: Alison Starling
Editorial Assistant: Emily Brickell
Art Director: Juliette Norsworthy
Design and Illustrations: Abigail Read
Photography: Tamin Jones and Kate Whitaker
Senior Production Controller: Allison Gonsalves